Straits Chinese

SILVER

A Collector's Guide

Straits Chinese
SILVER
A Collector's Guide

Ho Wing Meng

TIMES EDITIONS

The publishers wish to express their gratitude to Dr and Mrs Mariette for granting approval for their private collection to be photographed, without which *Straits Chinese Silver* would have been incomplete. And to Mr Peter Wee, who readily assisted at each photography session and contributed some items for photography, a note of sincere thanks.

Photography: First Photo Suppliers Pte Ltd
Cover design: Benson Tan

The first edition of *Straits Chinese Silver* was published in 1976 by University of Education Press, Singapore. This edition is based on a completely revised and expanded edition first printed in 1984.

Published by Times Editions–Marshall Cavendish
An imprint of Marshall Cavendish International (Asia) Private Limited
A member of Times Publishing Limited
Times Centre, 1 New Industrial Road,
Singapore 536196
Tel: (65) 6213 9288   Fax: (65) 6285 4871
Email: te@sg.marshallcavendish.com
Online bookstore: http://www.timesone.com.sg/te

Malaysian Office:
Federal Publications Sdn Bhd (General & Reference Publishing) (3024-D)
Times Subang
Lot 46, Persiaran Teknologi Subang
Subang Hi-Tech Industrial Park
Batu Tiga, 40000 Shah Alam
Selangor Darul Ehsan, Malaysia
Tel: (603) 5635 2191   Fax: (603) 5635 2706
Email: cchong@tpg.com.my

National Library Board Singapore Cataloguing in Publication Data
Ho, Wing Meng
    Straits Chinese silver : a collector's guide / Ho Wing Meng. – Singapore : Times Editions, c2004.
    p. cm.

Previously published: Times Books International, 1984
Includes bibliographies and index

ISBN : 981-232-757-6

1. Silverwork–Straits Settlements 2. Peranakan (Asian people) – Social life and customs   I. Title.

NK7179
739.237595– dc21   SLS2004011840

Printed in Singapore.

Contents

for
Fui Len
and
Alexis

Preface

The first edition of *Straits Chinese Silver* was published in 1976, just over eight years ago, and since then copies of that edition have virtually run out. Several publishers had therefore suggested that I issue a new edition of this book. I hesitated for some time, but finally agreed to the request, mainly because I had recognized for some time now, the need to critically revise the entire text as well as the illustrations, with a view to correcting some of the howlers, some factual errors, inelegancies of style, and include new information which had come to light in the course of the last several years. But for various reasons, I was unable to get down to work on the present edition until very recently.

Readers familiar with the first edition will notice that the present edition incorporates a number of improvements, including a wholly revised and expanded text, a larger format, and improved illustrations, many of the pieces having been re-photographed in colour. New items have also been included, representing some of the best of Straits Chinese craftsmanship. Where the illustrations are left in black and white, this was to highlight those scintillating qualities of silver which are better expressed in black and white rather than in colour.

These changes have been made possible by, among other things, the efforts and resourcefulness of a whole new generation of students and collectors in bringing to light a much larger variety of Straits silverwork than the meagre materials I had to rely upon during the early 'seventies. Not surprisingly, the better pieces of extant Straits silverwork are still held in private collections and not in the various museums throughout Malaysia and Singapore. This may be attributed to the fact that until the publication of *Straits Chinese Silver*, the actual provenance of these quaint-looking pieces of silverwork did not excite the interest or curiosity of students of antique Malayan arts and crafts. Except for H.N. Ivor Evans who had, in 1924, made some slighting remarks about the increasing presence of Chinese silverwork made in the Straits Settlements, most other scholars, including Frank Swettenham, deliberately ignored the existence of Straits Chinese silverwork. Even Ling Roth who illustrated several pieces of what we now know as Straits silverwork which he cryptically described as being of 'Chinese Design' or 'Chinese Origin' in *Oriental Silverwork* some seventy years ago, did not bother to mention the handiwork of local Chinese silversmiths. For this reason, perhaps, most scholars were led to believe that those pieces of silverwork found in Malaya sporting a blend of ancient Chinese motifs and Hindu-Islamic floral and foliated designs, had been crafted by silversmiths in China, and then brought out to Malaya by immigrants from South China.

Thus the burden of my argument in *Straits Chinese Silver* has been to show that this was a mistaken assumption, and that as far as the older generation of established goldsmiths and silversmiths in Malaya and Singapore was concerned, there was never any doubt in their minds that what I had described as 'Straits Chinese silverwork' was, in fact, the legacy of skilful silversmiths who once flourished in Malaya, particularly from the second half of the nineteenth century right up to the time of the First World War, when the Straits Chinese community was at its zenith of prosperity.

The realization of this fact was gradually brought home to us during the early 'seventies, in the course of frequent trips which my wife and I made to Johore, Malacca, Penang and parts of South Thailand, in search of silverwork and of old Chinese silversmiths who could enlighten us as to the origin of these fascinating, but fast-disappearing, crafts of a bygone era. Most of the surviving silversmiths whom we spoke to were emphatic in asserting that Straits Chinese silverwork, and even those pieces ostensibly made in Malay style, were either their own handiwork or else the products of their predecessors. What was even more convincing, we found at least a handful of old silversmiths still manually fabricating archaic hairpins, pendants, brooches, talismans and belts in the back-rooms of their shops.

The reception of *Straits Chinese Silver* has been more favourable than I dared to hope. But I am equally grateful to various people who took the trouble to review the book and offer critical comments, most of which have been very useful and constructive. No one, however, has contested the claim that works of Straits Chinese silver were the products of Chinese silversmiths resident in Malaya throughout the nineteenth century. I have not, therefore, thought it necessary to revise my thinking on this point, though I have re-examined, among other things, the provenance of some of those pieces which I had mistakenly attributed to the handiwork of local silversmiths.

Thanks to the spate of articles in popular magazines and local newspapers as well as exhibitions of Straits Chinese decorative arts in recent years, the educated public in Singapore and Malaysia has now acquired a better understanding and appreciation of the cultural heritage of the Straits babas. I would like to believe that *Straits Chinese Silver* played a little role in awakening interest in the material history of Malaya and Singapore.

It remains for me to thank all those kind and generous people who had contributed in one way or another to the writing of this book.

I wish to thank Dr. and Mrs. Mariette for their kindness in allowing me free access to their magnificent collection of Straits silverwork during the crucial stage in the preparation of the illustrations. Mrs. Mariette's enthusiasm was particularly infectious, while her illuminating observations on certain aspects of Straits silver saved me from some unsuspecting howlers. But most of all, I want to record my indebtedness to the Mariettes for kind permission to include some of their choicer pieces in the illustrations. If the present edition is a much improved version over the first, it is largely due to the inclusion of some of those remarkable examples of Straits Chinese craftsmanship *par excellence* from the Mariette's collection.

I thank Dr. Eunice Thio, formerly Professor of History in the National University of Singapore, for many past favours, not the least of which was to put me in touch with various people who own, or who know something about, Straits silver.

I am indebted to Mr. Peter Wee of Katong Antique House for permission to include several pieces from his collection in the illustrations, and for so many acts of kindness so willingly given during the preparation of this edition.

Mr. Teo Tee Hua, the photographer who took all the pictures illustrated in this book, deserves a note of appreciation for the special pains he took at all times to ensure that every one of his pictures was shown from the most effective angle and in the best possible light.

I also wish to express my appreciation to the following persons: to Miss Rosna Buang who patiently typed my manuscript several times over; to the Publishing Manager, the Editors and Book Designer of Times Books International for all the hard work they put into the production of this book; to Mr. Lee Liang Hye for checking and correcting my Malay spelling and for permission to reproduce several colour slides from his collection; to Mr. Lim Guan Hock of the Singapore National Archives for permission to reproduce some pictures of old Singapore and Malacca; to the General Manager of Times Periodicals; to Mr. Albert Teo; and to the late Mr. Andrew Lee.

As with my other work, *Straits Chinese Porcelain,* the first in the series on STRAITS CHINESE HERITAGE, this book is for my wife and son. At a time when nobody else had heard of such a thing as Straits Chinese silver, and when no museums in Malaysia or Singapore could be of any assistance to me either by way of information or specimen samples of Straits Chinese silver, my wife alone believed that the task I had set for myself was not a futile undertaking. It was with this conviction that she went about calmly ferreting out those articles which eventually formed the basis of my research materials.

Ho Wing Meng

1 Rediscovery of a Unique Craft

The largely unknown works of local Chinese silversmiths

THE HANDIWORK OF Chinese silver-smiths who flourished in the former Straits Settlement colonies of Penang, Province Welle-sley, Malacca and Singapore is largely unknown to most people, including students, connoisseurs and collectors of antique decorative arts and crafts found in Malaysia and Singapore. Outside these countries Straits Chinese silverwork has never been heard of. And until recently, very few people were aware that the majority of old silver artefacts found in old silversmiths, pawnshops and the homes of traditional Straits Chinese families some sixty or seventy years ago, but which are rarely encountered nowadays, were in fact the handiwork of *local* Chinese sil-versmiths. Many of these craftsmen originally came from China as far back as the eighteenth century, to make a living in the Straits Set-tlements. To people unfamiliar with the history and culture of the Straits Chinese, the prove-nance of these quaint-looking silver artefacts such as pillow and bolster ends (*buntal kepala* and *buntal pelok*), curtain hooks, betel-nut boxes and caskets (*chelpa, bekas sireh*), brooches (*kero-sangs*), belts and buckles (*pendings*), hairpins (*sanggul chuchuk*), pendants, anklets, etc., presents something of a problem.

This is because a typical piece of Straits silver, like everything else unique to the baba culture, as we shall see in the following chapter, is the product of a curious blend between the art and religious motifs of Chinese origin, and the motifs as well as the forms of articles derived from Hindu-Islamic culture. For this reason, it is not surprising that some otherwise knowledgeable collectors and dealers of local and Oriental antiques tended to ascribe Straits silverwork of local origin to the products of native silversmiths in South China, either because these artefacts looked typically Chinese, or because they believed that no local silversmith was capable of such craftsmanship. By parity of reasoning, experts were inclined to associate some equally authentic examples of Straits silverwork which were fabricated after the shapes of antique Malay objects of *virtu* and ornamented exclusively with floral and foliated motifs, with the handiwork of Malay or Javanese craftsmen.

Undoubtedly there are certain extant pieces of silverwork found in old family heirlooms which are of doubtful origin, particularly those un-marked pieces in which the workmanship is suffi-ciently ambiguous to justify the cryptic attribution 'possibly of Chinese origin'. But there

13

Fig. 1 The stark simplicity of the scrolled design in this Malay *buntal* plate (one of a pair) is equalled only by the severe and abstract quality of the floral motif it is supposed to represent. Nonetheless this is consistent with the precept of Islam which specifically forbids the realistic representation of animate things except in abstract and formalized patterns – in this case, all botanical connotations having been reduced to circles, ellipses, spiral segments, cones and parallel lines. Length: 19.5 cm. Width: 8.5 cm. From Johore.

is little doubt that the bulk of old silverwork, which was principally patronised by the Straits Chinese community, was made by many nameless, immigrant *sai pehs* (i.e., master craftsmen) who had acquired their skills from silversmiths in various parts of South China. We know for a fact that during the nineteenth century, soon after the founding of Singapore in 1819, thousands of craftsmen and artisans (including, naturally, goldsmiths and silversmiths) in China migrated to the Straits Settlements and other parts of Malaya where they settled down to practise their professions. One has only to talk to old, established goldsmiths and silversmiths who have been practising their craftsmanship for several generations either in Singapore or Malaysia to learn that up to about seventy years ago in Singapore, Johore Bahru, Malacca and Georgetown, it was common to find whole streets taken up on either side by rows of old-fashioned, two-storey shophouses (many elaborately decorated with dark teak or giltwood carvings) owned by Chinese goldsmiths and jewellers.

Although the writings of many British scholars

did not mention it, and there are no extant studies of any sort on the products of Chinese goldsmiths and jewellers in Malaya during the nineteenth century, it is certain that scholars such as Ling Roth[1], Frank Swettenham[2], H.N. Ivor Evans[3] and R.O. Winstedt[4] knew of the existence of locally-domiciled Chinese goldsmiths and silversmiths. For example, Ling Roth, who wrote the only standard work on old Malay silverwork which he praised very highly for their lovely and harmonious designs and craftsmanship (see fig. 1), noted in a rather matter-of-fact remark, that while in the case of Chinese silverwork the various motifs were executed with precision, their decorative designs tended to be marred by a complex of overcrowded, heterogeneous motifs. Indeed this overall impression of dazzling complexity and archaic quaintness probably made Chinese silverwork appear barbarous in the eyes of Europeans unfamiliar with the appearance of Chinese art motifs.

Winstedt, on the other hand, did not make any direct reference to Chinese silverwork, but it is possible that he had them in mind when he wrote

Fig. 2 This pair of rosette bolster plates is beautifully embossed with a variety of auspicious symbols consisting of a stag (symbol of longevity) in the central medallion, and the flowers of the four seasons interspersed with Taoist and scholarly symbols on the outer circular panel. Silvergilt. Diameter: 11.5 cm. From Singapore. Author's collection.

the following concerning old Malay silverwork: 'Islam which destroyed the Hindu art of Java, has done a service to the art of the Malay silversmith in restricting him to the conventional floral and foliated patterns *unspoilt by bizarre beasts and birds and naturalistic flowers*'⁵ (italics mine). It does not appear from this quotation as if Winstedt were comparing the simple elegance of old Malay silver with the products of either local or native Indian silversmiths, for these were not commonly encountered in Malaya. But the reference to 'bizarre beasts and birds and naturalistic flowers' (and Winstedt could have added 'grotesque figures') could very well have been applied to Straits Chinese silver which was full of such motifs including *ch'i-lings* (i.e., the Chinese unicorn or 'lion dog' as it is sometimes called), dragons (such as bald-headed dragons, winged-dragons, crocodile-dragons), antelopes, phoenixes, peacocks, quails, cockerels, cranes, fishes, bats, snails, squirrels, etc. As for Winstedt's reference to 'naturalistic flowers', there is a rich repertory of such motifs in Straits Chinese silver, such as, for example, lotuses, chrysanthemums,

peonies, plum blossoms, pomegranates, magnolias, grapevines, bamboos, lilies, plantains, etc. And all these, together with the rather grotesque figures of the Taoist immortals, lohans, arhats and bodhisattvas, form the vast inventory of auspicious and religious symbols found in Straits Chinese silverwork.

To the untutored eyes of most of these early English writers, the ornamental designs of Straits silver, with their complex juxtapositions of a wide variety of esoteric symbols, must have seemed bewildering, barbaric and decidedly repulsive (see figs. 2 & 3). What these writers did not perhaps realize, however, is that traditional Chinese art or, for that matter, much of ancient Oriental art, was essentially symbolic. The purpose of any object of Oriental art was primarily the expression of some religious belief according to certain accepted canons of propriety, and only secondarily the expression of the artist's personal sense of form and beauty. For this reason, then, most British scholars of Malayan culture found it hard to appreciate the strange and archaic qualities of Chinese silverwork.

Fig. 3 Of all the various artefacts made by local Chinese silversmiths during the nineteenth century for the baba-nonyas, those conspicuous ogival-shaped buckles shown here display most effectively that curious blend of traditional Chinese and Hindu-Malay art traditions. However, unlike Malay buckles (*pendings*) meant for commoners and royalty, Straits Chinese buckles do not vary in size – their average length and width being 14 cm and 11 cm respectively. From Malacca and Singapore. Mariette et al.

Fig. 4 The original caption to this postcard dated between 1900 and 1910 reads: 'Singapore: Chinese Dwelling Houses.' They were more than just Chinese townhouses; they were typical Straits Chinese homes. Notice that the ornate frontage of these houses displays a peculiar blend of Chinese and European architectural features. The European influence is clearly seen in the long louvred windows with rounded arches, stucco mouldings of flowers and 'Roman garlands', European wall and floor tiles and, some-times, ornate capitals for the supporting columns. The Chinese influence, on the other hand, is prominently displayed by those elaborate giltwood-carved doors, windows, banisters, huge lanterns and Chinese shop signs. Courtesy of the National Archives, Singapore.

But be that as it may, the curious fact about Straits Chinese silverwork is that although they were easily available in large quantities until about the 'twenties, practically nothing had been written about them nor, for that matter, about the fascinating culture of Straits Chinese community, and especially their womenfolk, the nonyas[6], whose fondness for ostentation made them the greatest patrons of Straits Chinese silver. Thus when I first chanced upon a few pieces of silver hairpins mounted with pearls (*sanggul chuchuk*) and pillow and bolster ends (*buntal kepala* and *buntal pelok*) in Malacca more than twelve years ago, nobody seemed to be able to say anything definite about the provenance and likely age of these articles, except that these came from old Straits Chinese homes (see fig. 4). Several elderly nonyas whom I consulted merely confirmed that these items of ornaments were commonly used by them up to the time of the Second World War. They were unable to volunteer much useful information other than the fact that they had regularly purchased their gold and silver orna-ments from their local jewellers and goldsmiths. The few surviving silversmiths in Johore and Malacca were, however, quite categorical in their assertion that these items of jewellery, and quite a few other things which they fished out from their drawers, were the handicrafts of bygone, locally-domiciled Chinese silversmiths. Others, especially the more chauvinistic of sil-versmiths (and I suspected these were the late-comers of the 1930s or the 1950s), insisted quite uncompromisingly that these old nonya artefacts were made *in* China formerly and exported to Malaya and other parts of Southeast Asia.

Since the information appeared to be conflic-ting, I decided to consult the relevant literature on the subject, hoping to glean some pertinent facts about these articles whose general design betrayed a strong influence of old Malay or Javanese silverwork, but whose decorative motifs were drawn very largely from the vast and varied repertory of Chinese art and religious symbols. As every student of Malayan history and culture knows, the most authoritative information was to be found in the comprehensive journals of the Malayan Branch of the Royal Asiatic Society. To my great disappointment, however, a thorough search through the *Cumulative Index* (1878–1963)[7] failed to elicit a single entry on anything remotely related to Chinese silverwork in Malaya. The only references under the heading of 'Silver' mentioned Kelantan silverwork, of which two articles, one by A.H. Hill[8] and the other by J.M. Gullick[9], appeared in the 1951 and 1952 issues respectively. A similar search in the Catalogue Section of the Main Library of the former University of Singapore was equally fruitless: no published materials on Chinese silver in Malaya existed.

Of course, there were the standard works on Oriental gold and silverwork, namely, that of Dr. Bo Gyllensvard's *Chinese Gold and Silver in the Carl Kempe Collection,* 1953, and Ling Roth's *Oriental Silverwork,* 1910. But Dr. Gyllensvard dealt exclusively with ancient works of gold and silver made in China for home consumption, while Roth was concerned mainly with old Malay silverwork found in Malaya. As for the handful of books and articles[10] which dealt with the history of Straits babas, their customs and traditions, no mention was ever made of those conspicuous fineries of gold and silver, namely, large ogival-shaped buckles with elaborately hand-wrought belts, impressive brooches, elegant hairpins, earrings, bracelets, pendants, necklaces and anklets which their womenfolk, the nonyas, were wont to display on ceremonial occasions.

British historians who wrote about the customs and ceremonial etiquettes of the Malay royalty often expressed admiration for the quiet elegance and craftsmanship of Malay, as well as Sumatran and Javanese silverwares, which invariably graced the courts of the rajahs and sultans as insignias of royalty. This inherited preference for old Malay and Indonesian silver is very clearly reflected in the fine collections of old silverwares in the National Museum of Singapore and Frank Swettenham's bequest of Malay silver in Muzium Negara in Kuala Lumpur. The National Museum's collection is notable for its inclusion of Sumatran, Brunei, Thai and even old Balinese silverwork, while the Swettenham collection consists exclusively of old Malay silverwares. It is in the charming little State Museum of Penang that the student of Straits Chinese culture really finds a small but representative collection of old Straits silverwork. But even here the collection has been augmented only in recent years.

As for the State Museum of Malacca, where one would have expected to find the most comprehensive collection of Straits Chinese silver, it is disappointing to report that during the early 'seventies, in the initial stages of my research, the only examples exhibited were a few 'Portuguese hairpins' (so-called because they were reputedly worn by Portuguese nonyas), two or three brooches of indifferent workmanship, and several anklets of Malay origin. The dusty and yellowing labels merely identified these articles without divulging any other relevant information.

Fig. 5 This is a view of the mouth of the Singapore River showing the busy traffic of Chinese junks, lighters and bumboats which regularly commuted between ships lying in the Inner and Outer Roads of the Singapore harbour and the string of warehouses situated along Boat Quay (on the left of the picture) and Havelock Road. This picture was taken at the turn of the present century. Courtesy of the National Archives, Singapore.

Why the study of Straits Chinese heritage was neglected

This deliberate omission and neglect of Straits silverwork, or, for that matter, all the other decorative arts of the baba community, in the collections of the more important museums of Malaysia and Singapore, as well as in the records of historians and students of Malayan arts and crafts, is all the more remarkable when one considers the fact that the babas have been living in Malacca continuously for six hundred years. And what is more, from about the second half of the nineteenth century, many Straits Chinese merchants and trading families throughout the Straits Settlements went on to amass great fortunes and became very influential in the affairs of Penang, Malacca and Singapore. Yet if we examine the various circumstances which influenced the opinions of those early writers of Malayan affairs, we can perhaps understand why the cultural heritage of the Straits babas had been neglected for so long.

To begin with, the majority of these early writers appeared to have been far more interested in the customs, traditions and local history of the indigenous Malays rather than the cultural history of the Malayan Chinese who, in any case, were never regarded as the true natives of the country. Besides, most of the early Chinese who came to settle in Malaya were largely merchants, traders, artisans and labourers. Few, if any, belonged to the *literati* class. And however quaint or fascinating the arts and crafts of immigrant Chinese craftsmen might have been, they reflected at best the cultural traditions of an alien people. Added to this is the fact that what little some of the early English writers wrote about the Chinese in Malaya during the nineteenth century was largely misleading, often biased and rarely favourable. In his description of the Chinese in Malaya, for example, T.J. Newbold[11] stereotyped them as selfish, ardent lovers of money, inveterate gamblers and opium addicts. In the same way, J.D. Vaughan, an astute observer of the customs of the Penang babas, committed what to many prominent peranakans of the time, was an unpardonable blunder of failing to distinguish between the Straits-born Chinese and the China-born Chinese, when he indiscriminately lumped them all as 'chinamen'.[12] The babas were particularly offended by Vaughan's sweeping statement to the effect that the Chinese, as a rule, were given to gambling, making money (by ruthless means) and getting involved in subversive secret society activities. It was perhaps too much to expect of some of the more obtuse colonial officials who happened to think only in stereotypes that the Straits-born Chinese were ethnically and culturally different from the rest of the 'chinamen'; and it took them quite a long time to realize that the Straits babas had a distinctive culture of their own.

There was, I think, another feature of Malay silverwork which readily caught the attention of those early British colonial officials: silver was a precious metal exclusively reserved for members of the Malay royalty to fashion such articles as their ceremonial regalia, items of personal jewellery and household utensils, much in the same way that silver utensils had traditionally been used by the royal and aristocratic classes in England and Europe. For this reason, those showy salvers, enormous trays, boxes, bowls, personal jewellery and insignias of upper-class nobility, such as huge buckles and elaborately crafted belts, medallions, necklaces, headgear, krises and sceptres, had to be made large and impressive so as to enhance the status and dignity of the sultans and their royal consorts.

Thus, apart from the fact that the Malays had what the immigrant Chinese lacked, namely, aristocratic traditions, Malay silverwork had the advantage of being exclusively associated with the Malay royalty. This, in the eyes of those snobbish and status-conscious colonial officials and British writers, conferred additional prestige and value to these articles both as works of art and as objects of cultural significance.

Straits Chinese silverwork, by contrast, was relatively insignificant, not merely in the sense that they were never made for royal use or court ceremonies (there being no personage of imperial lineage among the predominantly merchant community of babas), but also because Chinese silverwork had always been confined to articles of *virtu* and items of personal jewellery. It is true that the sophisticated and affluent nonyas of Penang, Malacca and Singapore were no less fond of ostentatious display of wealth and finery than the female members of the Malay royalty. And in the days gone by, it was customary for the wealthier nonyas to commission all their items of jewellery in gold, rather than silver, and mounted with diamonds, rubies, sapphires and emeralds. Silver and silvergilt articles mounted with baroque pearls and a variety of rough-cut industrial quality diamonds from Kalimantan, were used only by those who could not afford to have their jewellery in gold and high-quality precious stones. *But, and this is what distinguishes the Straits Chinese from the Malay royalty, the nonyas preferred to have all their luxury articles small, precious-looking and finely crafted. Whether the article is of silver or gold, the emphasis was always on the quality of the workmanship – not the magnitude of the article.* For this reason students of Straits silverwork or gold will look in vain for giant buckles as much as 30 cm in length.

Apart from their diminutive characteristic, articles of Straits Chinese silver were turned out in large quantities during the latter part of the nineteenth century, and this fact may explain why nobody really felt that local Chinese silverwork deserved any notice at all – at least not until the 'sixties of the present century when they had largely disappeared from traditional Chinese gold- and silversmith shops in Penang, Malacca, Johore and Singapore. Malay silverwork, by contrast, had always been a scarce and luxurious commodity, reserved only for Malay royalty.

If British scholars of Malayan affairs took little notice of Straits Chinese silverwork, Chinese scholars and antiquaries took *no* notice at all of their own gold and silver artefacts, not even with regard to the finest of Chinese gold and silverwork made during the T'ang Dynasty (A.D. 618–906). This is because the traditional bias among the *literati* class in China required that the decorative arts should be relegated to the category of 'minor arts'. For this reason, Chinese scholars and collectors in Malaya never paid any attention to the products of the jeweller's vocation, whether they are of Straits Chinese or native provenance. Indeed the traditional Confucian snobbery about literary and scholastic achievements dictated that the proper interests of the scholar-gentleman should be confined primarily to an intimate acquaintance with the writings of Confucius and Mencius, and only secondarily to the art of painting and calligraphy.

With the exception of jade perhaps, everything else which was associated with manual work was considered menial and frowned upon. For this reason, even the best of Chinese silverwork have never acquired the kind of reputation and esteem which English or French silver have established with connoisseurs of European art.

Nonetheless, the disappearance of any ancient form of native art or craft once admired for its beauty and craftsmanship will, sooner or later, be viewed with regret by people of discriminating taste. This nostalgia for the arts of a bygone age is not simply a sentimental reaction. It springs from a deeper and perhaps better appreciation for the aesthetic and cultural values of those things which have now come to be regarded as the heritage of a nation.

With regard to old Malay silver, the time-honoured craft of the various households of the rajahs and sultans of various states in Malaya, it was practically moribund by the closing decades of the nineteenth century. Both Roth and Evans pointed out that many of the traditional Malay craftsmen found it increasingly difficult to make a decent living in the face of stiff competition from imported European silver and silver-plated articles, as these imported products found increasing favour in the Malay courts. Since the royalty were virtually the sole patrons of Malay silversmiths, declining royal patronage forced many of these craftsmen out of their profession. The more intrepid continued to fabricate silverwork, but soon found the competition from immigrant Chinese jewellers too tough for their continued survival. With their characteristic drive and capacity for sustained hard work, Chinese goldsmiths and silversmiths could turn out every conceivable article made by Malay craftsmen with equal dexterity, if not artistry, in a shorter time, and at prices which were well within reach of the increasingly affluent wives of Straits Chinese merchants and traders throughout the Straits Settlements.

Thus with the demise of old Malay silverwork, the business of Chinese goldsmiths and silversmiths throughout Malaya went on to prosper for many more decades, as mounting wealth among the Straits Chinese merchant and trading classes created greater demands for the products and services of the jewellers and goldsmiths. But by the third decade of the present century, with the onset of the Great Depression from 1929 to 1933, even the days of the Chinese goldsmith and silversmith were numbered.

There were other social factors at work, too, which eventually spelt the death-knell for the gold and silverwork which catered to Straits Chinese tastes. These included (i) the increasing effects of English education and, with it, the adoption of Western lifestyles, especially in dressing; and (ii) changes in outlook brought about by conversion of an increasing number of peranakan Chinese to Christianity, such as the abandonment of many of their traditional practices regarding weddings, funeral services and ancestral worship.

Now the traditional Chinese goldsmith and silversmith, who had catered to the needs of the baba-nonyas all along on matters pertaining to jewellery and ornaments for the elaborate wedding ceremonies, came gradually to discover that demands for their once highly-prized handicrafts began to take an irreversible downward plunge from which they never recovered. And with the passing away of many of the older generation of master craftsmen, and the reluctance of the younger generation to perpetuate a dying tradition of craftsmanship, many of the surviving goldsmiths and silversmiths sold out their family establishments or switched to other forms of business.

This monograph is intended to be an essay in the description and appreciation of an obsolete craft of the Straits Settlements era. It is also an attempt to add a little to our knowledge of a largely neglected, and until now unknown local craft, of which only the vestiges survive among old family heirlooms of peranakan homes, private collections and a few museums in Malaya and Singapore. More importantly, perhaps, my aim is to describe the role which these objects played in the customs and traditions of the peranakan Chinese of the nineteenth century. I have therefore deviated somewhat from the normal practice of writings on art, namely, an exclusive concern with technical descriptions about the category of art in question, with particular reference to such characteristic features as uniqueness of shape and design, age and provenance. Without detracting from the importance of these considerations, I have nevertheless adopted the somewhat unorthodox method of treating the subject of Straits Chinese silver from the standpoint of the cultural uniqueness of the babas in order to shed some light on the peculiar characteristics which typify the products of old Chinese silversmiths.

Fig. 6 This is part of the frontage of another Straits Chinese-type house at No 12, Kampong Hulu, Malacca. It was built for Mr. Tan Koh Poh, a wealthy rice merchant at about the time of the First World War, according to his daughter-in-law. The present descendants of Mr. Tan informed me that Mr. Tan Koh Poh had wood-carvers and carpenters specially brought in from Fukien Province, South China, to carve all the interior panellings and partitions. Courtesy of Mr. Tan Kee Gak.

Only against the cultural setting of the Straits Chinese community do these small but showy artefacts acquire their real significance as a distinctive style of Chinese silverwork whose unique characteristics are equalled by the remarkable singularity of the baba culture itself.

The definition of Straits Chinese silver

Finally, a few words must be said about the definition of the term 'Straits Chinese silver'. The qualifying expression 'Straits Chinese' or, if you prefer the more colloquial expressions, 'peranakan Chinese' or 'nonya' silver, must *not* be understood to imply that these ornamental objects were fashioned by craftsmen drawn from the peranakan community. On the contrary, many of the babas from the late eighteenth right

through the nineteenth century, belonged either to the class of wealthy merchants and traders, or to that of the landed gentry (see fig. 6). From the end of the nineteenth century to about the time of the Second World War, the majority of their male descendants in particular took to white-collar, clerical jobs in the British colonial civil service. True to the Confucian tradition of snobbery, the babas had always despised manual labour. Those locally-domiciled goldsmiths and silversmiths who created the great bulk of what I have called 'Straits Chinese silver' were, almost without exception, non-peranakan of conservative Chinese extraction, who adhered strictly to the ancient customs and manners of their forefathers in China. They were drawn mainly from the Hokkien and Teochew communities, and in the majority of instances (so a number of still-surviving silversmiths aver) they acquired their skills from master craftsmen in China, or else from local craftsmen who originally came from the Kwangtung or Fukien Provinces. After the founding of Singapore in 1819, many of these craftsmen migrated to the Straits Settlements where they eventually settled down to practise their crafts.

The term 'Straits Chinese silver' or simply 'Straits silver' as sometimes used in this book, therefore, refers exclusively to certain unique characteristics of locally designed silverwork which, in the days gone by, was almost exclusively patronised by the nonyas of the peranakan Chinese community. The stylistic peculiarities of Straits silverwork are worth noting because, as will be seen in the illustrations, the shapes and forms of some of these articles are entirely alien to, and absent from, the entire repertory of traditional Chinese silverwork made for home consumption. These include pillow and bolster plates, betel-nut boxes and cups, hairpins, necklaces, brooches, earrings, finger-rings, ogival-shaped buckles and matching belts and wire-work purses. These articles, crafted as they were with traditional Chinese art and religious motifs, are nonetheless so *un-Chinese in shape and function*, that some otherwise knowledgeable local antiquaries, when first confronted with these artefacts, could not help feeling perplexed when called upon to identify the real provenance of these artefacts.

They could clearly see for themselves that the decorative designs, usually executed in familiar chased or repoussé work, consist of recognizably Chinese art and religious motifs, these being the flowers of the four seasons, the emblems or figures of the eight Taoist immortals, the dragon,

the phoenix and the *ch'i-ling*. Occasionally, the presence of stamped marks in Chinese characters describing the purity of the metal, or perhaps the shop-names of the silversmith, also proclaims the true origin of these artefacts. Nevertheless these experts, who had presumably never heard of the Straits Chinese babas, were at a loss to explain why the shapes and designs of these articles were so alien to conservative Chinese tastes. Indeed, one old silversmith in his late seventies, when shown a few of these nonya hairpins, appeared rather amused and casually remarked in Hokkien: 'Only *siaw kaw* (literally "mad dogs") wear such baubles!' One venerable collector of impeccable tastes simply refused to recognize these pieces of silverwork as Chinese in origin, notwithstanding the presence of Chinese inscriptions or the evidence of traditional Chinese motifs in these artefacts. He maintained quite categorically that these articles were of Malay or Javanese origin – the marks of Chinese characters being forgeries!

If the task of identifying the true provenance of Straits Chinese silver had been made difficult, until recently, by the conspicuous lack of research and published materials on the subject, the traditionally biased attitude of some chauvinistic antiquaries, as well as the ingrained tendency of many people to venerate imported articles more highly than locally crafted ones, did not make the task of the student of Straits Chinese material culture any easier. For when we first tried consulting several antique dealers of old jewellery concerning the origin of some *buntal* plates, curtain hooks and buckles sporting Chinese art motifs executed in typical repoussé work, they eagerly assured us that these were products of *sai pehs* in China – with additional innuendos to the effect that China-made silverwork was worth higher prices!

Since there was, for several years, no independent evidence to the contrary, we accepted the opinions of antique dealers until, quite by chance, we encountered several old silversmiths living in semi-retirement in some obscure little towns in Malaysia, who intimated that some of these artefacts had been fabricated by them and their predecessors way back in the nineteenth century. Some of these craftsmen were still at work making belts, hairpins, pendants and talismans. Several of these silversmiths even offered to sell us samples of their handiwork made fifty or sixty years ago stamped with their own shopmarks. One obscure goldsmith in a little village-town in Malacca showed us a beautiful set of twenty-eight hairpins made in the shape of phoenixes which, he claimed, were crafted by his deceased father and bearing his shopmarks, many years ago. It was unthinkable, he said, for him to part with these hairpins, because he had a sentimental attachment for his father's handiwork; but from time to time, he would hire them out to Malay royalty for use during the *bersanding* (wedding) ceremonies. Until about ten or fifteen years ago, the jewellers and goldsmiths along Chulia Street and Beach Street in Georgetown, Penang, were regularly fabricating exquisite pieces of Penang nonya-style pendants, brooches, earrings, finger-rings and hairpins.

While the provenance of Straits Chinese silver is no longer a matter of pure conjecture, it is still difficult to distinguish certain categories of Straits silver from the products of South China silversmiths who traditionally operated from Hong Kong, Canton, Swatow, Amoy and Shanghai during the nineteenth century. This is because all Chinese silversmiths, whether they hailed from South China or Malaya, were trained in the same tradition, while ingrained conservatism ensured that the forms and decorative designs of Chinese silverwork everywhere shared a great degree of family resemblances. However, from about the second half of the nineteenth century when Hong Kong, Canton and Shanghai silversmiths began to turn out silverwares intended for European markets, the shapes of these articles (e.g., coffee and tea services) were naturally fashioned to suit the tastes of European clients. The decorative designs of these wares, however, remained essentially Chinese and included such well-tried motifs as peonies, lotuses, chrysanthemums, plum blossoms, phoenixes and birds on foliage, dragons, flower baskets, insects, etc. Chinese silversmiths also attempted to imitate the English system of assaying hallmarks by stamping their articles with their shop-names both in Chinese characters and English alphabets denoting their initials, together with such numerals as '80', '85' and '90' to indicate the degree of purity of the metal employed. Occasionally, the words 'Hong Kong' and 'Shanghai' may appear on the bases. Date-marks, however, were never employed.

These, then, are the distinguishing characteristics which differentiate South China export silverwares from Straits Chinese silverwork. The local variety of silverwork, it must be remembered, was never intended for export to European markets, and so, as far as the shapes of such utensils are concerned, one would rarely find in the entire repertory of Straits silverwork articles such as tea and coffee services, cigarette boxes, cocktail shakers, trophy cups, salvers or silver forks and spoons. Besides Straits silver articles are never stamped with English alphabets denoting the initials of the maker, nor the use of English numerals to indicate the purity of the metal employed.

The difficulty of attribution arises only when we encounter silver articles which, to all intents and purposes, resemble similar pieces known to have been made by Straits silversmiths, not only in the overall design but also in the technique of execution. By and large it was not customary for South China silversmiths to fabricate articles whose shapes were characteristically Hindu-Islamic in inspiration, not because they were incapable of turning out such articles, but because native Chinese silversmiths were unfamiliar with their shapes and functions. Besides, we know of no record or evidence of any sort to show that gold and silver artefacts specifically intended either for Malay royalty or the womenfolk of wealthy Straits Chinese merchants during the nineteenth century had ever been made by craftsmen in China. For this reason, we are fairly certain that typically Straits Chinese silverwork such as those·large and ornate ogival-shaped buckles, European-styled pendants, brooches, bracelets, betel-nut boxes, pillow and bolster plates were the products of local silversmiths.

A lost art

The study of Straits silverwork is especially timely and pertinent as these artefacts have now largely disappeared from antique shops and old silversmiths throughout Malaysia and Singapore. The supply of old silverwork has dwindled to a point; before long the few remaining dealers in antique silver would either have to close down or diversify into other forms of merchandise. In fact this once thriving craft of ancient lineage became obsolete over half a century ago when most of the Straits Chinese became converted to Christianity and Western lifestyles.

This, and the fact that goldsmiths and silversmiths (not to mention the innumerable pawnshop owners) had regularly melted down great quantities of gold and silver articles during the last eighty years or so, accounts largely for the current rarity of Straits silverwork. The inherited bias of former museum curators for old Malay and Javanese silver has also contributed in no small measure to the conspicuous absence of the handiwork of local Chinese silversmiths in museum collections throughout Malaysia and Singapore. And last, but not least, the decline and dispersal of the peranakan community which, for nearly two hundred years, constituted the most wealthy and influential group of Chinese in Malaya, probably sealed the fate of this time-honoured craft. In the remaining pages, therefore, I shall try to identify some of the crucial factors which led to the cultural decadence of the unique baba ways of life, from the latter part of the nineteenth century, to about the time of the Second World War.

Just as the Straits babas had been the first community of overseas Chinese in Malaya to assimilate Malay customs and traditions to suit their own special needs, so, too, they had been second to none in their enthusiasm to adopt English education and English values and lifestyles. This was clearly manifested by the fact that the babas were among the first to send their sons to local English schools during the nineteenth century, even though privately endowed Chinese schools were available in Malaya in those days. Those from the wealthier Straits Chinese merchant class even sent their sons to be educated in expensive private schools in England. The brighter ones who made the grade were even given the rare privilege of furthering their studies in London, Cambridge and Oxford Universities.

In the beginning the conservative baba merchants were quite content to allow their children, while they were in England, to cut off their long Manchu-style queues in favour of westernized, shorter hairstyles. They also permitted their sons to put on English costumes, attend church services, and even profess Christianity. But as soon as these anglicized and educated young men returned to their homes in Penang or Malacca, their elders insisted quite uncompromisingly that they reverted to the traditional customs of wearing Chinese costumes (Manchu costumes for men and *sarong kebaya* for women). They had to renounce Christianity in favour of Confucianism, and by

and large, to faithfully observe the customs of their forefathers.[13]

However, at about the turn of the present century, the situation had changed considerably. More and more peranakan children, especially the boys, had already been to local English schools, and English education was regarded as the prerequisite for anyone seeking admission to the ranks of the colonial civil service. In the meantime, Christianity had also become more acceptable to the younger generations of westernized babas, thanks to the missionary zeal of the Christian brothers, nuns and other evangelists of the Christian schools.

As the more 'enlightened' among the younger generations of babas readily assimilated English values and lifestyles, this gave them, among other things, the opportunity to discard some of the more irksome and meaningless rituals which their elders had dogmatically imposed upon them. In this, however, the more 'progressive' young babas and nonyas discovered that, but for the deep respect which their elders had for the *orang puteh* (i.e., white man) and the powerful influence which he wielded in the affairs of government, it would have been virtually impossible for them to set about modernizing their traditional outlook and ways of life. English education, in particular, held promise of white-collar jobs in the civil service; and before long, it came to be regarded among English-educated babas who had attained what in those days was called 'Senior Cambridge Certificate' of education, that the most normal career anyone could aspire to was that of a *krani* or

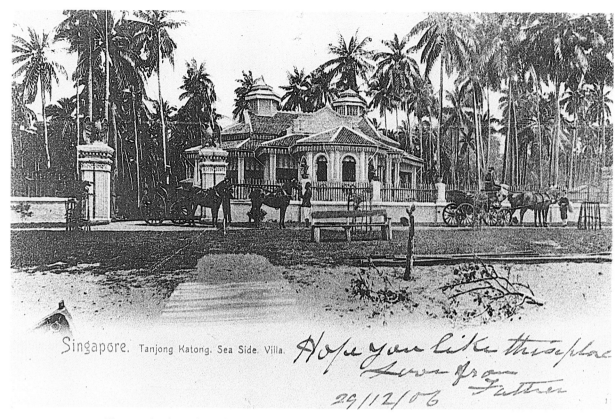

Singapore. Tanjong Katong. Sea Side. Villa. *Hope you like this place Love from Father* 29/12/06

Fig. 7 This huge bungalow house was sited along the East Coast of Singapore and belonged to a wealthy Straits Chinese family. Up till about 1950 or so, many of these spacious bungalows could still be seen stretching all the way from Tanjong Rhu to Bedok. This particular house, featuring a curious blend of European and Malay architectural structures, was sited on the grounds of a large coconut plantation. The two horse-drawn carriages with attendants indicate that this picture was taken before the advent of motorcars, that is, around 1910. Courtesy of the National Archives, Singapore.

clerk in some government department. For the more affluent young men who also happened to be more brainy, there was nothing more desirable than a career in the legal profession. In those days, to be called to the bar was a signal achievement for any ambitious young man; and in the eyes of his parents still steeped in the traditions of ancient China, this was equivalent to acquiring the status of *kuan* (i.e., official or magistrate) in the imperial service of the court. It is not mere circumstance, therefore, that some of the most prominent peranakans of the Straits Settlement era were lawyers, magistrates and judges in the legal service of the colonial government.

Thus the most notable characteristics which distinguished the babas from the other Chinese communities in Malaya from about 1870 onwards to about 1950, was their undisguised admiration and high regard for the English civil servants and officials of the colonial govern-

ments; and they therefore sought to emulate English manners and ways of living (see fig. 7) wherever they could afford to do so. This attitude of unreserved veneration contrasted sharply with the Straits babas' sentiments of derision and mild contempt for their China-born money-grabbing compatriots, the *sinkehs*. The *sinkehs*, for their part, did not share what they regarded as a sycophantic veneration for the superiority of the *orang puteh*, his culture and system of values. Nor, for that matter, was the China-born merchant class disposed to acknowledge political allegiance to the British government represented by its colonial governors. Indeed, they regarded themselves as itinerant merchants and traders for whom the Straits Settlements were but temporary trading posts, providing lucrative business opportunities. It was to China and the teachings of her ancient sages which they looked to for inspiration, guidance and wisdom. The babas, on the other hand, had become so assimilated to the local culture and traditions of the native Malays over the centuries, that the teachings of Confucius, Mencius and Lao Tzu, not to mention the accumulated knowledge and wisdom of Chinese civilization, were closed books, inaccessible, and in many important respects, meaningless.

It seems clear, then, that with the passage of time, the adoption of English customs and system of values and the Christian religion, inevitably led the babas to abandon their distinctive mode of life, their ancient customs and traditions, and along with these things, to reject those elaborately crafted articles of gold and silver which had been so intrinsic to their customs and practices. For example, conversion to Christianity dealt a fatal blow to one of their most important institutions, namely, those elaborate ceremonies associated with Straits Chinese weddings. The substitution of traditional Straits Chinese customs with Christian wedding ceremonies meant that the bride and groom no longer had to don their magnificently embroidered costumes, their gold and silver articles of jewellery such as the ornate, coronet-like head-dress, barley-twist bracelets, glittering hairpins, multi-stranded necklaces, anklets, earrings, finger-rings, etc. The presentation of exquisitely crafted silver *sireh* sets, ornate pillow and bolster plates, ornamental gewgaws for the bridal bed – all these, and many other lovely things, had to be discarded from the bridal trousseau. As for the adoption of Western bridal gowns for the bride, and suits for the bridegroom, this meant that those elaborate and impressively crafted gold and silver buckles with matching belts had to be abandoned; while the use of key-holders, purses, brooches, silver and beaded purses, etc., had become obsolete.

Is it any wonder, then, that the significant decline for the products of the traditional Chinese silversmith led to the eventual demise of this time-honoured craft? The problem of declining demand was to some extent aggravated by the import of mass-produced substitutes of silverwares from Britain such as Sheffield plate, EPNS and sterling silverwares. As was to be expected, the wealthy Straits Chinese merchants began to patronise British and European manufactured wares and other decorative objects. Many among the older generations of Straits Chinese can still recall that during the heyday of British supremacy, any article stamped or marked with the 'Made in England' label was greatly esteemed for its real or imagined guarantee of quality. Whether it was the gleaming finish and perfection of Sheffield plate or EPNS products, or simply the fashionable preference of British technology which captivated the imagination of the traditional babas, it is not easy to say. But emulating the customs and lifestyles of the British colonial civil servants became such a favourite pastime with the more well-to-do babas that, by the opening decades of the present century, the traditional Straits Chinese culture was no longer what it used to be. What many people did not perhaps realize at the time was this: that rapid erosion of the ancient customs and traditions of the Straits Chinese was to have wide and adverse repercussions, not the least of which was the total disappearance of the art of gold and silver craftsmanship of nineteenth-century Singapore and Malaya.

2 Lifestyle of the Straits Chinese

THIS IS A good juncture at which to draw attention to a largely unrecognized fact about the tradition of babas of the former Straits Settlements, namely, their cultural uniqueness among the various communities of immigrant Chinese in Malaya. By and large English writers, even those who had been regarded as noted authorities on Chinese affairs from the nineteenth century to the present, appeared to have ignored, if they had not been actually ignorant of, this fact. Even Victor Purcell, the well-known author of that standard work on the Chinese of Malaya,[14] did not, at any time, take the trouble to explicate the distinctive characteristics of the Straits babas which, in some fundamental ways, set them apart from other Chinese communities in Malaya. He must have known, however, that in spite of all their superficial ethnic and cultural affinities with other dialect groups, the peranakan ways of living and thinking were so distinctive as to set them apart as a different ethnic group altogether. Like all other English historians, however, Purcell seemed to have assumed that the various communities of overseas Chinese residing in Malaya could, to all intents and purposes, be lumped together as members of a culturally homogeneous group of people, the Han Chinese.

While this may be true of the majority of the China-born *towkay* or merchant class as well as the class of petty traders and artisans who adhered uncompromisingly to ancient Confucian customs and traditions, who spoke their own dialects and insisted upon an exclusive Chinese system of education for their sons, the same cannot be said of the Straits Chinese. It is true that some of the Hakka, the Hainanese and the Cantonese families have been living in Malaya for at least four or five generations. But unlike the peranakan Chinese who had readily adopted the customs and practices of the native Malays, these conservative Malayan Chinese groups had rigidly kept to their ancient ways of living. The Straits babas were alone unique in being the only community of immigrant Chinese who spoke a Malay *patois* known as 'Baba Malay'; and for as long as anyone can remember,

Fig. 8 This picture shows a wealthy and influential Chinese wearing the heavily-embroidered robe of a high-ranking Manchu official – the large square badge on his chest indicates that his status was that of one of the thirteen categories of court officials. During the nineteenth century all Chinese 'Kapitans' of the Straits Settlements were allowed to don one of these official robes provided they paid a high fee to the government of China, and many wealthy overseas Chinese merchants made it a habit to buy the right to wear these impressive robes for the purpose of impressing upon their local compatriots their new-found status. But after 1911, with the collapse of the Ch'ing Dynasty, it became increasingly rare for wealthy local business tycoons (including the babas) to wear such robes on ceremonial occasions. Courtesy of the National Archives, Singapore.

they adopted and modified the traditions of the native Malays to suit the peculiar needs of their own community; so that what eventually came to be recognized as 'Straits Chinese culture' or 'Baba culture' was really the product of the fusion or intermingling of customs and traditions of the early Chinese settlers and the native Malays.

To begin with, and this may probably come as a surprise to some, the traditional, Malay-speaking babas, born and bred in Malacca, never really looked upon themselves as Chinese at all.[15] The Malay term *china* (or Chinese) and its pejorative equivalents, *sinkehs* (meaning 'newcomers' or 'country bumpkins') and *china-tok-tok* (slang for China-born Chinese) were expressions which the babas used when making slighting or derogatory references to the habits and manners of the working-class Chinese whom they despised. To the sophisticated peranakan Chinese accustomed to a long tradition of courtesy and refinement of manners, the coarse and rustic habits of the working-class *sinkehs* were irritat-

ingly disagreeable; while snobbery about wealth and social status enjoyed by their forefathers, some of whom had been made Kapitans (see fig. 8) by the Portuguese, the Dutch and then the English, made it impossible for them to regard these immigrant, working-class Chinese as anything other than menials. Thus the *sinkehs*, who originally came in great numbers as barefoot, contract labourers, seamen, artisans and petty traders to the Straits Settlements, were perhaps as alien to the babas as the Japanese, Koreans or Vietnamese.

Now this reluctance to identify themselves as Chinese rather than *peranakan* (i.e., Straits-born) is not to be attributed to ignorance on their part concerning the common racial origin which the babas shared with the *sinkehs* in Malaya. On the contrary, they were perfectly aware of their racial origin as they were proud of their long and continuous association with the chequered history of Malacca and the achievements of their forefathers, some of whom had contributed munificently to the development of the Straits Settlements. But they recognized what many people did not, that during more than half a millenium of continuous residence in Malacca, they had been cut off from the mainstream of Chinese civilization. Consequently, they had evolved a distinctive culture which incorporated many Malay (and perhaps Portuguese and Dutch) customs into the main corpus of Chinese traditions. It was, until the coming of the British during the nineteenth century, a sort of hybrid culture which was un-Chinese in some fundamental aspects without its being, at the same time, a sort of neo-Malay culture. For, as will be seen in the following pages, the Straits Chinese never wholly adopted the customs of the Malays without modifying them to suit the peculiar needs of their community.

It is not without reason that the peranakan Chinese felt offended whenever Englishmen referred to them as 'Chinamen', a term which, in 'the good old days' of British imperialism, was used indiscriminately and pejoratively to refer to any Chinese who happened to profess the mandarin attire, sport a long Manchu queue and observe typically Chinese customs. The babas objected to the term 'Chinamen', not only because they had little in common with *sinkehs* in respect of the language they spoke (and the babas spoke mainly Baba Malay and English), their customs and practices, but also because they had never been known to profess any political or cultural attachment to China.[16] Unlike the *sinkehs*, they did not make any effort whatsoever to inculcate in their children a love and

reverence for the things which had always been universally valued in China, namely, the ability to read and write Chinese characters, the acquisition of an adequate knowledge of Chinese literary, historical, social and philosophical values as part of the indispensable intellectual accoutrement of every scholar-gentleman. It is true that some of the early settlers who made good in the Straits Settlements used to send their sons back to China for their education. But in those days education was the privilege of a very small and wealthy minority. The majority of young babas either acquired a smattering of English education or remained illiterate for the rest of their lives. For the majority of home-bred Malacca babas, therefore, the system of values which they cultivated was largely a blend of obsolete Chinese traditions and local Malay customs and folklore which were handed down by oral tradition from father to son.

With the coming of the British to Malaya during the nineteenth century, English education at primary and secondary levels became available for the first time to all His Majesty's territorial possessions. To the surprise of most people, the babas took to English education with an alacrity which was quite unthinkable either to the native Malays or, for that matter, to the conservative *sinkehs* who, for more than a century afterwards, continued to view English education with a mixture of contempt and suspicion. No true and loyal Chinese, in their opinion, would forsake the language and cultural values of his fatherland for the language of the *yang kuei* ('foreign devils' that is!) and its

Fig. 9 The frontage of the Yong Chun Huay Kuan (a 'Huay Kuan' in Hokkien simply means 'association') in Jalan Tun Tan Cheng Lock, Malacca. The author is standing in front of the impressive doors painted with the figures of some Chinese deities. There are many such Chinese associations scattered throughout Singapore, Malacca and Penang. Courtesy of Mr. Lee Liang Hye.

Fig. 10 This is the somewhat neglected frontage of the Tan Kim Seng ancestral family home in Heeren Street, Malacca, as it is today. The gorgeously carved giltwood *pintu pagar* or front gate has disappeared. The house is now deserted and in a somewhat dilapidated state – the descendants of Mr. Tan no longer live here. It is being looked after by a rather dour and sullen caretaker. However the ancestral altars and photographic mementos of Tan Kim Seng and his equally illustrious son, Tan Jiak Kim, are still to be seen – moulding away and worm-eaten. Photo courtesy of Mr. Lee Liang Hye.

concomitant system of values, so utterly different from his own. And so, in order to keep alive the Chinese language and the hallowed traditions of Confucianism in a foreign country, the richer and more successful *towkays* formed *kongsis* or associations (see fig. 9) not only for the protection of their own interests, but also for the purpose of setting up private schools dedicated to disseminating Chinese education for all Chinese children throughout Malaya and Singapore. Even today there are many Chinese schools and institutions of learning in many parts of Malaysia and Singapore which are largely financed by various groups of wealthy Chinese merchants and businessmen. As for the Straits babas, they showed not the slightest enthusiasm for sending their children to Chinese schools. The Mandarin tongue did not appeal to them at all. They preferred English education because, among other things, it guaranteed white-collar jobs in the colonial civil service.

As far as the Straits Chinese were concerned, neither China nor her well-tried system of values held any special esteem for them, because they had never known any other home except Malacca and its surrounding regions. Equally, they were unfamiliar with any other system of values except the unique peranakan traditions which their forefathers had evolved as a result of six hundred years of residence in Malacca. Thus it was regarded as perfectly natural that many enterprising and successful peranakan merchant-traders such as Mr. Tan Kim Seng and Mr. Tan Chay Yan who had found their Eldorado in Singapore, should finally decide to retire in the quiet town of Malacca where they might spend the rest of their days among the quaint and picturesque Chinese houses in the vicinity of Heeren Street (see fig. 10) and Jonker Street, or perhaps in one of those spacious, Portuguese-Dutch houses along Limbongan, Klebang Besar or Tanjong Kling.

Fig. 11 This is a scene of the Malacca River as seen from a high pedestrian bridge located behind the site of the present Pasar Besar (the Central Market) and looking towards the mouth of the river. Parts of the banks near the mouth of the Malacca River, as it stands today, were built up of large, weather-worn red laterite stones, which were in all probability taken from the ruins of Fort Famosa built by the Portuguese during the sixteenth century. Courtesy of the National Archives, Singapore.

To the traditional Straits babas, therefore, Malacca rather than China was their fatherland; and as for the famous Malacca River (see fig. 11) which still winds through the Town Centre, but hardly attracts any attention at all, it was a waterway of great historical significance, especially to the older generations of babas before the turn of the present century. Through its muddy and meandering course in the days of yore, Chinese junks used to come sailing in, conveying not only boatloads of merchandise from China and the surrounding countries, but also their humble forebears, many of whom came barefooted and penniless in search of a haven far from the privations of wars and famines which periodically ravaged China.

Many of those early traders and immigrants who came to Malacca and subsequently travelled to Penang and Singapore, stayed on for the rest of their lives. The more enterprising, those gifted with great business acumen, went on to make substantial fortunes for themselves. The others who did not attain spectacular financial gains went on to lead a better standard of living than they had ever dreamed of in China.

The distinctive baba culture that we know of today is the product of a long evolutionary process of cultural assimilation. It began when some of those early, itinerant Chinese traders, who came to Malacca during the early fifteenth century, began taking native girls for their spouses. Since the children of these intermarriages grew up in homes where their mothers spoke not only Malay, but also practised Malay customs, it was a matter of time before a community of Malayanized Chinese appeared on the scene, speaking a peculiar Malay *patois* and practising a set of customs which was a curious blend of ancient Chinese and Malay practices. To the subsequent generations of peranakan Chinese cut off from the mainstream of Chinese civilization, therefore, Malacca became the focus of all their sentiments,

Fig. 12 View of the *rumah abu* (ancestral home) of the Tan Kim Seng family in Heeren Street, or what is now known as Jalan Tun Tan Cheng Lock, Malacca, as seen from across the palatial house of the Chee family. The narrow frontage (about 30 feet) of such old Canton-styled shophouses belies the depth and spaciousness of the interior – sometimes stretching by as much as 250 feet. Since Mr. Tan Kim Seng retired to Malacca after a lifetime of business and philanthropic activities in Singapore in the 1850s, this house may be dated to about that time. Photo courtesy of Mr. Lee Liang Hye.

Fig. 13 This richly-carved giltwood *pintu pagar* (front gate) of Mr. Tan Koh Poh's house at No 12, Kampong Hulu, Malacca, is one of the few Straits Chinese-styled gates to be seen in Malacca. The carvings are executed on both the obverse and reverse sides of the gate. See fig. 6 for the reverse side. Courtesy of Mr. Tan Kee Gak.

while Bukit China, Bukit Gedong and Bukit Tempurong, constituting some of the largest burial grounds outside China, from the seventeenth century up to the present, bear witness to the bond of attachment which they had always felt for this charming, old-world corner of Malaysia.

Therefore some of the superficial manifestations of cultural affinity between the peranakan Chinese and the China-bred Chinese in Malacca before the Revolution of 1911 in China, such as the Confucian code of ethics, the costumes of the males or even the Manchu queues all Chinese wore, not to mention the typical Chinese shophouse (see fig. 12) dwellings of the peranakans in Heeren Street and Jonker

Street, are in fact misleading and deceptive. Many of the things peculiar to the babas, including, particularly, the Canton-styled houses they lived in, with pagoda-like eaves and tiles, the typically Chinese ornaments and decorative motifs which characterized their carved, giltwood doors (see fig. 13), windows, screens and panels, were undoubtedly of Chinese inspiration and workmanship. But if you ask any average latter-day baba or nonya in Malacca for the meanings of the various carvings and gilded characters on their doorfronts and windows, if you ask for an interpretation of the various art and religious symbols used in the carved panels, you will soon discover that they cannot read the characters, let alone unravel the deeper significance of the mystic Taoist and Buddhist symbols. Neither does the average baba speak Mandarin though some may speak the Hokkien or Teochew dialects. Indeed these traditional Chinese art symbols in peranakan homes are the vestigial mementos of a bygone era whose import has been lost to them, mainly as a result of the Straits Chinese having assimilated the language and culture of the local natives during the course of six hundred years of residence in Malacca.

Now this sense of cultural uniqueness with which the babas prided themselves was reinforced by an accident of history, namely, the creation of Malacca along with Singapore, Penang, Province Wellesley and the Dindings as Crown Colonies of the Straits Settlements in 1826. Under this new political set-up, all persons born here would legally be eligible to claim rights and protection due to them as 'British subjects'. As was to be expected, the babas welcomed the prospect of becoming British subjects with enthusiasm, as this would, among other things, help to dispel their traditionally dubious political status. Whereas the China-born immigrants in Malaya steadfastly refused to regard themselves as subjects of the British government, the babas regarded their new-found status as a badge of recognition which they greatly coveted.[17] For such was the admiration the babas had always felt for the authority of the British government that they would much rather be British subjects than citizens of the Republic of China.

Fig. 14 This is a reproduction of an original water-colour painting of the harbour at Georgetown, Penang, by a certain Captain H. Cazalet. It was painted in 1856. The British authorities in Calcutta had hoped that the acquisition of Penang as a British Crown Colony in 1786 by Francis Light, would provide a base for refitting ships of the English East India Company during their long voyage (lasting nearly two years) from London to the Far East and back. Here we see several 'East Indiamen' (so the ships of the East India Company were called) and a Chinese junk lying at anchor in the harbour of Georgetown. Courtesy of Katong Antique House.

Fig. 15 This is a scene of Collyer Quay (about 1910?) which most Singaporeans have never seen before. All the buildings on the right have long since disappeared. Notice that, except for the electric tram which ran on overhead trolleys (centre), there were no motor-cars – only horse carriages and rickshaws (foreground). Courtesy of the National Archives, Singapore.

Language

From a very early period of their history, the babas of Malacca adopted a corrupt form of the local Malay dialect known as 'Baba Malay' as the language of communication between them and the native Malays with whom they traded. The evolution of Baba Malay was greatly facilitated by intermarriages between the early Chinese traders and the native Malaccan girls; as time went on, the growing community of Malayanized, or peranakan Chinese, spoke fewer Chinese dialects among themselves, until Baba Malay became virtually the *lingua franca* of the town. Even today there are many babas and nonyas in Malacca and elsewhere in Malaysia who speak only Baba Malay – not even any one of the commonly spoken Chinese dialects such as Hokkien, Teochew, Cantonese, Hakka or Hainanese.[18]

According to the Reverend W.C. Shellabear[19] who spent many years living in Malacca, Baba Malay is a form of Bazaar Malay liberally supplemented and modified by a large collection of Hokkien words in its vocabulary. For example, to anyone familiar with this dialect, the Hokkien roots of the following words in Baba Malay are unmistakable: *chêngteng, tok, kongsi, locheng, loteng, sampan, sinkeh, sênsé, pô-hô, chinkeh, tau-hoo, koyok* and *chat*. Their vocabulary of purely Malay terms is relatively limited, while the syntax of sentences was largely derived from the Chinese language rather than the original Malay written and spoken by the natives. When-

ever new words were required, they would be coined directly from the Hokkien or Teochew vocabulary.

Few babas learnt to read or write in Jawi (the classical Malay script which resembles Arabic), and except for those who took the trouble to learn Bahasa Melayu, the babas did not speak Malay after the manner of the natives. Indeed some even described classical Malay as *Melayu hutan* (meaning 'Jungle Malay'). They preferred their own *patois* of Malay suitably modified by Hokkien syntax and vocabulary because it sounded better to their own ears, though understandably ludicrous to a Malay. For example, the babas, according to Shellabear, used the possessive particle *punya* far more often than is appropriate, one example being: "Dia **punya** mak-bapa ada dudok makan di s'blah **punya** meja".

As the traditional babas did not learn to read and write either Jawi or the romanized Malay script, they were largely ignorant of the great body of Malay literature and were without a written language of their own. Hence this explains why there were no written records of, say, the history or evolution of their community, their cultural values and literary works by peranakan writers, despite the fact that their community had been in existence for six hundred years.[20] It is a well-known fact, however, that the babas had their own dramas (most of which had been composed extempore and committed to memory) and a rich collection of *pantuns* or ballads, of which Sir Cheng Lock Tan, a prominent Malaccan baba, was said to have been an accomplished reciter.

Fig. 16 This picture shows some of the rare books in Baba Malay published and printed in Singapore. These books were not written by the Straits babas themselves; they were merely translations of popular ancient Chinese classics rendered in the peculiar *patois* of the Straits babas, namely, Baba Malay. The earliest translations were done by some bilingual Chinese or baba translators, of whom the most well-known were Chan Kim Boon (better known by his pen name Batu Gantong) and Pang Teck Joon, and they were published in the 1880s. The last of these publications went out of print after 1938. Courtesy of Times Periodicals.

Pantuns

Strictly speaking, the traditional *pantun* is, according to R.J. Wilkinson's definition, 'a quatrain the first line of which rhymes with the third and the second line with the fourth'. It can draw upon any variety of topics, be it about love, beauty, sorrow, wisdom, 'the dirty old man' or the wicked mother-in-law! It is sung to the accompaniment of one tune repeated with variations by the violin, a couple of rebanas, a brass gong and, occasionally, an accordion. According to Mr. Gwee Peng Kwee, an eighty-year-old doyen of the Gunong Sayang Association of Singapore, a Dondang Sayang (or *pantun* singing) session starts off with the leading *pantun* singer reciting the opening theme. He does this by first singing the entire quatrain followed by a repetition of the first and third line and then the second and fourth line. Having done so, he retires to the side and a second singer takes over. The second singer can, if he so chooses, add to

or rebut what the first singer had sung. From then on, anyone who is quick-witted enough can enter the 'fray'. According to Mr. Gwee, there is something particularly 'infectious' about extemporizing *pantuns*: the recitation of one quatrain often leads to ideas for a second quatrain, a third, a fourth and so on. On this question of the infectiousness of improvising *pantuns*, the background music provided by the violin, the rebanas, the gong and the accordion is particularly helpful. It stimulates the *pantun* singer to 'hatch out' new ideas, while allowing a certain interval of time to formulate an effective repartée. Indeed, an evening session of Dondang Sayang usually lasted till the wee hours of the morning, when every *pantun* singer had virtually exhausted his or her skill in composing *pantuns*.

In 'the good old days' *pantun* singing was an essential part of the elaborate Straits Chinese wedding ceremonies, and it was not unusual for quick-witted and quick-tongued guests to try to pit their skills in composing the most amusing *pantuns* for an evening of entertainment. To

Fig. 17 An early photograph of a Straits nonya wearing the traditional *baju kurong*, the national costume of the nonyas until about the time of the First World War (1914–18) when it was supplanted by the more modern-looking *sarong kebaya*. Judging by the three ear-pick type of hairpins (of which only two are visible in this photograph) used by this lady, we may infer that she is a nonya of Malacca or Singapore origin. Courtesy of the National Archives, Singapore.

ensure that the enjoyment of *pantun* recitations did not pall, there were frequent interruptions for sessions of *joget ronggeng,* a popular form of Malay dancing in which everybody was encouraged to participate. Unfortunately, *pantun* recitation and *ronggeng* dancing have now become obsolete. Younger generations of Malay youths prefer disco dancing!

Attire

Although language was the most important component of the Malay culture which the peranakan Chinese had adopted as their medium of communication, they espoused quite a few other Malay customs and practices which, as usual, they appropriately altered and innovated upon to suit the special needs of their community. For example, until about the end of the last century, the Straits Chinese males continued to observe that age-old custom of wearing typically Chinese costumes consisting of a loose-fitting, long-sleeved silk or satin tunic with square-cut collars and ankle-length skirt slitted at the sides. They also wore long Manchu queues, black skull caps, velvet shoes, and, after the manner of the Chinese gentleman-scholar, held a semi-circular fan in one hand.

With regard to the female attire, however, they tended to be more liberal in their attitude. From an early period of their history, they permitted their womenfolk to adopt a variation of the Malay dress known as *baju kurong* (fig. 17), which the nonyas referred to as *baju panjang,* as the standard costume to be worn on all important social functions other than the wedding ceremonies. The costumes worn by the bride and groom on their wedding day are usually made of heavily embroidered damask silk or satin materials and the designs are traditionally Chinese in style. Basically, these consist of a two-piece suit comprising an oversized, long-sleeved, T-shaped coat matched with an ankle-length, pleated or slitted skirt. The most striking feature of these exorbitantly expensive costumes is the splendour of the ornate embroidered designs worked into the fabric. Indeed a complete set of wedding costumes for the bride, the groom and two child-attendants could cost several hundred dollars about eighty or ninety years ago.

Now the *baju kurong,* as worn by the nonyas until about the opening decade of the present century, consists of a long-sleeved, knee-length blouse which is open in front, and a hand-printed batik *sarong* made of fine cotton. The two frontal hems are secured together not by buttons, but rather by a set of three round silvergilt or gold brooches studded with pearls and other precious and semi-precious stones. The *baju kurong* was the standard attire of all nonyas, both young and old, and it only went out of vogue when the *sarong kebaya* became fashionable at the turn of the present century. The younger nonyas then took to wearing the more elegant *sarong kebaya* while the older generation of nonyas adhered to the *baju kurong.*

The *sarong kebaya* costume is similar in overall design to the *baju kurong,* except that instead of the knee-length blouse, the modern *kebaya* was shorter and reaches down to below the waist. It is usually made of muslin-like or voile fabrics and elaborately embroidered with floral and foliated patterns along the hems and the lower portions of the blouse. Since the material for the *kebaya* was a thin, muslin-like fabric, it was usually worn over an inner cotton vest-coat which, in the days before the invention of the modern brassieres and corsets, served a similar function. Nowadays the *sarong kebaya* is the standard costume of all nonyas.

The nonyas also adopted and modified another Malay custom, namely, their style of hairdressing. Indonesian and Malay women generally comb their hair backwards to form long tresses which are then twisted and turned into a large, loose bun, not unlike the shape of a doughnut, at the back of the head, and secured by small metal clips and pins. Usually the bun is also adorned with some highly-scented white flowers such as *bunga melor* or *bunga tanjong.*

The Straits nonyas, on the other hand, comb their hair very tightly backward to form a long plait which is held together by the application of a watery glue, and then twisted into a small, tight top-knot positioned high on the back of the head. This top-knot is much smaller than the looser hair-buns worn by Indonesian and Malay women and hence given the name of *sanggul siput,* but there is a broad stem of hair which issues from the lower back of the head. The top-knot which the older generation of nonyas sported was usually decorated by three remarkable-looking hairpins of graduated sizes – the largest being about seven inches long, with a bolt-like crown, was inserted right through the top-knot. The second and third hairpins may be of similar design, but are shorter and smaller. Sometimes the nonya used hairpins of a different design, namely, those with a tapered stem, the broader end of which is soldered with a spray of flowers executed in pierced work and mounted with pearls or roughly-shaped industrial diamonds from Pontianak in Kalimantan Island. The second hairpin was usually inserted at a right angle to the first, and the third inserted just below the second. Like their Indonesian and Malayan counterparts, the Straits nonyas inserted jasmines and other fragrant flowers into their hair-buns.

Since the blouse of the *baju kurong* and the *kebaya* blouse of the *sarong kebaya* were always

Fig. 18 Four ceremonial combs used by traditional nonya brides – the top right-hand piece sports a decorative panel of gold. Except for the piece on the top left, the rest of the combs are made of tortoise-shell and sheathed with gold or silver panels ornamented in chased and repoussé work. Length of longest comb: 6 cm. From Singapore and Penang. Mariette collection.

matched to a batik *sarong*, the wealthier nonyas secured their *sarongs* by using an elaborately designed silver or silvergilt hand-crafted belt held in position by an impressive buckle. These belts and buckles were not only functional, but were among the most impressive articles of personal adornment.

As for the *kebaya* which was usually embroidered with birds and floral motifs in colourful silk threads along the edges and lower parts of the blouse, the frontal hems are secured together with a set of three *kerosangs* or brooches joined together by chains. Each of these brooches (usually made of silvergilt or gold) is fashioned after the shape of a leaf with serrated edges. The decorative design inside the leaf consists of flowers and leaves done in pierced work and mounted with diamonds, pearls, emeralds or other precious stones in *à jour* settings. The cheaper *kerosangs* of

silvergilt were usually mounted with coarse, industrial diamonds which display a quiet sort of glitter.

Sireh-chewing

Chewing of *sireh* leaves and tobacco is another ancient Malay custom originally derived from the habits of the Tamils of South India who, as early as the seventh or eighth century of the Christian Era, sailed to Malaya to trade with the natives of the coastal states of Kedah and Perlis. Later on they established permanent settlements along the banks of rivers flowing into the Indian Ocean and the Straits of Malacca. The peranakan Chinese, it may be noted,

Fig. 19 A typical Straits Chinese *sireh* set showing the lidless rectangular box made of purple sandalwood and inlaid with mother-of-pearl, floral motifs, and the four *sireh* containers and *sireh* cutter. Notice that there is a little drawer at the lower part of the box: this drawer is used to hold *sireh* leaves. The lobed silver caskets are of exceptional quality: the motifs are carved out of solid silver panels and then appliqued to the sides and covers of the caskets. The ormolu trimmings are of nine-carat gold. Mark of 'Ching Fu'. From Penang. Mariette collection.

are alone among all the other Chinese communities in Malaya, in adopting this native Malay habit of chewing *sireh* leaves and even tobacco.

The method of preparing *sireh* is as follows: a piece of *sireh* leaf is selected and applied over with a thin layer of quicklime paste over the centre portion. Some fragments of gambier (an astringent extract from the gambier tree) are then added to the top of the lime to be followed with several slices of areca nut. The leaf is then folded into a neat rectangular bundle and slipped into the mouth. In the days gone by, it was customary to offer *sireh* and tea to one's guests as a gesture of hospitality, and no important social function went by without the presence of that ubiquitous *tempat sireh* (i.e., a lidless rectangular box of lacquer or silver with four little caskets and cups usually ornamented with fine chased or repoussé designs) being passed across the table from guest to guest. The only un-Malayan aspect of this formality is the serving of *sireh* **and** tea.

In all the years that I have been observing the habits and manners of the Straits babas, I have never heard it said that the traditional peranakans were connoisseurs of tea-drinking. Nonetheless the remarkable thing about the older generations of Straits Chinese is that they used to brew their tea in small, elegant-looking porcelain teapots and would serve them in dainty teacups – a practice reminiscent of the style of brewing and serving tea employed by the *literati* class of ancient China! And anyone who has had the opportunity of rummaging among the *bric-à-brac* of old baba homes will discover some of these dainty-looking teapots and stacks of complementary teacups.

In any case, the peranakan Chinese always served tea in little porcelain cups, never out of large cups or even mugs. This is because the proper way to savour the finer varieties of Chinese tea was to take the brew in small sips and not large gulps. In Malay customs, however, *sireh*-chewing was never accompanied by tea-drinking, and generally, the Malays preferred coffee to tea as the common beverage of the natives. Incidentally, *sireh*-chewing was mainly a nonya habit; the men did not, as a rule, chew *sireh* leaves, except perhaps, in Malacca, where it is said that some babas made it a habit to chew *sireh* leaves.

Nonya cuisine

After *sireh*-chewing, nonya cuisine is another notable feature of the peranakan culture. There is no doubt whatsoever that the distinctive nonya food evolved when the Malay wives of those early Chinese traders, way back in the fourteenth and fifteenth centuries, introduced native dishes in Chinese homes. But like everything else about Straits Chinese customs, the purely Malay styles of food preparation underwent gradual changes over the centuries as they were modified to suit the palate of the Malayanized Chinese. It is not my purpose, within the

Fig. 20 The picture shows two typical Straits Chinese dishes, namely, the Babi Pong Tay (bottom) and Chicken Curry (top). According to Ms Violet Oon (see her *Peranakan Cooking*, Times Periodicals), these two dishes were ideal for informal parties, and particularly during the Chinese New Year, because they could be prepared several days ahead. The Babi Pong Tay is pork stewed with garlic, soy sauce, fermented soybeans (taucheo) and sugar. Courtesy of Times Periodicals.

limited scope of this chapter, to discuss in any great detail the highly specialized and complex subject of nonya cooking, except in very general terms.

The most distinctive feature of nonya cooking, to my mind, is the incredible amount of labour invested in the preparation of the various dishes. The procedures are time-consuming, tedious and complex, and the cook herself must be gifted with a discriminating sense of taste and smell if she hopes to turn out mouth-watering dishes! Actually there is nothing very special about the kinds of ingredients used in the preparation of standard nonya dishes. These include the common spices such as onion, garlic, turmeric, white ginger, lemon grass and other aromatic leaves, tamarind, pepper, chilli, nutmeg, cloves, cinnamon and coconut. The Malays, Indonesians and South Indians use the same types of spices. But

nonya food differs from others in the time-consuming methods of preparation, the liberal use of coconut milk in their curries and gravies, and the blending of traditional Chinese dishes with Malay styles of cooking. The nonyas make frequent use of a hard paste of crushed shrimps known as *belachan* which has an offensive odour for some people. But *belachan* is an indispensable ingredient in nonya food because it adds a special flavour to the already spicy dishes. Even when strictly Chinese dishes are required, such as for example, pork cooked in black soy sauce or duck cooked with sour, preserved vegetables, the nonyas would invariably add their own concoctions of fragrant and spicy seasonings to give an added tang to these otherwise mild dishes. From the peranakan point of view, food which is neither spicy nor hot (chilli hot that is) is considered unsavoury (see fig. 20).

This preference for spicy and piquant flavoured food is another distinguishing characteristic which set the Straits babas apart from other Chinese of immigrant stock, particularly, the conservative Cantonese, the Teochews, the Hakkas, the Hainanese and the Hockchias, many of whom do not eat other types of food except those which conform to their own well-tried methods of cooking. Among the more modern generations of English-educated Chinese, however, contacts with the Straits babas gave them the opportunity to sample their unusual culinary preparations, and the majority of them soon acquired a taste for nonya food which they came to appreciate far more than their own bland Chinese dishes.

Until about ten years ago, there was a real danger, in the minds of many discerning people in Singapore, that the fine art of nonya cuisine would be lost beyond recall when older generations of surviving nonyas pass from the scene. This concern for preserving an ancient culinary art of a unique but fast-disappearing breed of people, was given further credence by the fact that most modern women of Straits Chinese stock no longer practise the fine art of cooking in which their mothers and grandmothers excelled. This lack of interest is attributed to the fact that the pressures of urban life leave little time and leisure for the working woman to spend long hours in the kitchen turning out tempting dishes. It was felt, therefore, that unless some people took the trouble to put down in writing the knowledge (and secrets) of nonya cooking, this art could be lost forever.

Thanks to the efforts of the late Mrs. Lee Chin Koon, Mrs. Ellice Handy, Mrs. Leong Yee Soo, Miss Violet Oon, Mr. Terry Tan and a few other enthusiastic exponents of nonya cooking, the endangered art of Straits Chinese cuisine has now been preserved through the publication, in recent years, of a number of cookery books exclusively devoted to expounding this esoteric form of food preparation.

Wedding practices

Last but not least, Straits Chinese wedding customs and practices should be mentioned because they are characterized by a fascinating blend of old Chinese and local native practices in their various ceremonies. Since it is not possible nor desirable to describe in lengthy detail the marriage customs of the peranakan Chinese or the meanings of all those elaborate procedures in a book of this sort, it will suffice to note that although the peranakans adhered quite conservatively to Chinese traditions, there were obvious traces of Malay influences in their wedding formalities (see fig. 21). For example, in old baba customs, three days before the wedding day, the groom's family would send twelve attendants bearing gifts to the bride's family. Following what was apparently a Malay custom, these gifts were all placed either on brass or red lacquer trays (the Malays in Peninsular Malaya preferred brass trays while the *bataks*

Fig. 21 The bride and groom shown here (Mr. and Mrs. Chong Pak Sen) are modernized peranakans. But they opted to don the traditional but richly embroidered wedding costumes of the Straits Chinese when they were married on 29 November 1978. The only unusual feature of this picture is the way in which the bride was asked to pose standing at attention with her arms by her sides, instead of the traditional pose which required the bride to fold her arms in front of her. The result was that the oversized embroidered sleeves of her upper garment looked clumsily cavernous for her tiny hands! Had she posed with the arms folded in front of her, the ornate embroidery on the sleeves would have been shown in the best possible light. Courtesy of Katong Antique House.

Fig. 22 This triangular piece of ornament made of velvet and cotton backing and embroidered with small metal beads, small appliqued silver ornaments and an ornate band of florets and tassels, is known as *sapu tangan* in Baba Malay. It was worn on the fourth finger (there is a little ring attached to the apex) by the bride, on the third day of her wedding. Length: 20 cm. From Penang. Mariette collection.

of Sumatra used magnificently crafted red lacquer ones), and were ceremonially carried to the bride's ancestral home known in Malacca as *rumah abu*, to the accompaniment of strident Chinese music produced by the seronee or *lah-pah* – a trumpet-like instrument – and the beating of brass gongs.

The contents of these trays, it is interesting to note, besides containing the usual Chinese foodstuffs such as dried sea-slugs, birds' nests (not the literal thing but rather a jelly-like substance which a species of bird produce by vomiting), mandarin oranges, chickens, ducks and a roasted pig or portions of it, also include a piece of *kain songket* (a type of fabric hand-woven out of gold, silver and coloured silk threads by traditional Malay weavers) and several *ang pows* or gift packets wrapped in red paper. The first of these *ang pows* should contain twelve dollars known as *wang tetek* (nursing money); the second *ang pow* containing a larger sum of money, say, one hundred dollars was called *wang belanja* (expense allowance); and a third *ang pow* known as *wang sireh* (betel-nut money). There was also a tray containing the marriage agreement (written in Chinese or romanized Malay) called *surat kahwin*. The final touch of Malay influence was to be found in a tray containing some yellow-dyed betel-nuts and a comb of *pisang raja* (a variety of bananas known as 'royal bananas'). When the groom formally called upon the bride's home on the wedding day with his retinue of relatives, seronee musicians and attendants carrying umbrellas and lanterns, he was invariably accompanied, close to his side, by a Pak Chindek,

a Malay master-of-ceremonies dressed in Malay costume.

These and the recitation of *pantuns* and *ronggeng* dancing, reflect more than just the superficial influence of Malay culture. In all other respects, though, formalities of Chinese origin were observed, such as the swearing of fidelity to each other, the bowing and offering of joss-sticks at ancestral altars of the bride's and groom's homes, the partaking of *kway-ee* (a sweet made of glutinous rice dumplings dyed red and boiled in *gula melaka* soup), drinking tea, presenting eggs, sugar cane, rice wine and red candles.

One can go on describing many other interesting features of baba customs such as, for example, the religious practices, their lavish New Year ceremonies, birthdays, their dramas, etc. in order to underline the Sino-Malayan characteristics of their culture. But enough has already been said to show what a remarkable culture the babas had evolved, and why, for this reason, the history and culture of their community should find a proper place in the annals of Malayan history instead of being conveniently forgotten. It is not often realized that the evolution of the baba community which, unfortunately, was already on the decline even before the Second World War, was not one of those accidents of history which flashed into the limelight, and just as swiftly disappeared into the oblivion of time. In fact, it had its humble beginnings six hundred years ago when some seafaring Chinese traders and merchants from South China first decided to use Malacca as their trading post in the East Indies.

Fig. 23 The Gate of Famosa or Porta de Santiago, Malacca: this was all that remained in 1807 after the British had systematically shot down the formidable wall which once surrounded the inner enclave of Fort Santiago originally begun by Alfonso de Albuquerque, the conqueror of Malacca during the sixteenth century. The low, white-washed wall to the left of the Gate is not part of the original wall which was much higher and made of large, red laterite stones now pitted and weathered by age. This photograph was taken at the turn of the present century. Courtesy of the National Archives, Singapore.

By the time the great Portuguese commander, Alfonso D'Albuquerque, sent Captain Sequeira to reconnoitre Malacca in 1509 with the intention of capturing the city by force of arms, and which he did subsequently in 1511, Sequeira found that the friendly Chinese traders had already preceded them by at least one century (see fig. 23). According to the official records of the Ming Dynasty, *Ta Ming Hui Tien,* the coming of the Chinese may be dated to the arrival in Malacca of a huge armada of armed Chinese junks under the command of Admiral Cheng-ho, who had been sent by the Ming Emperor, Yung-lo (1403–24) to the court of Parameswara, reputedly the founder of Malacca, in 1409.[21] However, there is an ancestral tablet in Malacca which states that a certain Captain Li Chi-t'uan, a native of Lu Kiang in Fukien Province, left his home in the beginning of the Ming Dynasty (which officially commenced in 1368) and eventually settled in Malacca. With him came other Chinese traders from Tsing Chin Wan near Amoy and San Tau.[22] If this ancestral record is true, it means that the earliest Chinese immigrants came to Malacca about forty years before the arrival of Admiral Cheng-ho.

According to Mr. Yeh Hua Fen,[23] however, some of the oldest graves in Bukit China, Bukit Gedong and Bukit Tempurong may be dated as far back as the sixteenth century, if not earlier. But because of the state of decay suffered by some of these tombstones, the inscriptions are no longer legible; so it is impossible to confirm the existence of fifteenth- or even fourteenth-century graves. However, Mr. Yeh points out that there is a gravestone in Bukit China belonging to a Kapitan 'Nya' and his wife, and it bears the date of the Emperor 'Lung Wu' (I think Mr. Yeh meant Lung Ch'ing [1567–72]) of the middle Ming period. With the exception of this solitary gravestone bearing a sixteenth-century date, the majority of early graves with authenticated datings are attributable to the closing decades of the Ming Dynasty (i.e., between 1600 and 1644); and this fact is corroborated by the records of the oldest families in Malacca, namely, the Tans, the Tays and the Lis.

3 The Characteristics of Straits Chinese Silver

Shapes and decorative designs

GOLD AND SILVER articles have always been regarded by the peranakan Chinese as status symbols. But by and large, most of the pieces which they commissioned from the local goldsmiths and silversmiths were confined to items of jewellery and some ornamental articles and utensils specifically intended to give that added touch of luxury and glitter to their already ornately furnished homes. While the Straits babas admired the British style of gracious living, they did not attempt to emulate wholesale the practice of English upper-class nobility by ordering sumptuous dinner services or splendid tea and coffee sets made of sterling silver to grace their homes and impress their guests on all formal occasions. Similarly, there were no such things as massive salvers, monteiths, tankards, goblets, tureens and candlesticks of silver in Straits Chinese homes; and because the traditional peranakan Chinese adhered very closely to ancestral worship, such silver objects of religious ceremonies in the Christian churches, namely, crosiers, monstrances, reliquaries, custodia, chalices and patens are totally absent from Straits silverwork.

Indeed their enthusiasm for silver or silvergilt artefacts did not go beyond articles intended for personal ornament, objects of *virtu* and occasional pieces of trophies, commemorative bowls, little wine ewers, teapots, pillow and bolster plates, curtain hooks, little vases and *sireh* boxes. True to conservative Chinese tastes, the peranakan Chinese preferred to have their most important and impressive household ornaments and utensils made of *porcelain;* in the days gone by, it was not unusual for the wealthier of Straits Chinese merchants to spend considerable sums of money on porcelain wares, some of which were ordered direct from Ching-tê-chên in Kiangsi Province. These included some grandiloquent vases, ornamental jars, goldfish bowls, flower pots, drum seats, bridal basins, incense burners and large covered jars. The Straits babas also bought huge sets of dinner and tea services sometimes running into thousands of pieces painted to their specifications, namely, phoenixes and peony blossoms rendered in polychrome enamels. Porcelain wares painted in this unique style are now referred to as 'Straits Chinese porcelain' or, more colloquially, 'nonya ware', and for more detailed information on the subject, the reader is referred to my book *Straits Chinese Porcelain.*

It is worth noting here that to the babas as well as to the traditional Chinese, serving food and drinks out of porcelain containers was an ancient tradition stretching back to a thousand years ago when true porcelain was first discovered some time during the T'ang Dynasty (A.D. 618–906). Therefore they had no reason to imitate the Europeans by switching to large dinner and tea services of *silver*, when porcelain wares, particularly those specially commissioned imperial wares, were so much appreciated as objects of refinement and sophistication. Besides, silver plate suffers from one grave disadvantage, namely, that vessels of this type heat up very rapidly, so that when food and drinks are served hot (and the Chinese have always insisted that their food and drinks be served piping hot), it is practically impossible to handle, say, a bowl or a cup without being well and truly scorched in the process.

Now as everybody knows, the traditional Chinese eat their food out of a bowl containing rice or porridge with the help of a pair of chopsticks. These chopsticks, despite their ungainly appearance, serve a dual function. Firstly, they can be easily manipulated to pick up morsels of meat, fish, vegetables and other delicacies from the various dishes on the table, and secondly, they facilitate the scooping of the contents of the bowl into the mouth when it is brought close to the lips. Of course proficiency in the manipulation of the bowl and chopsticks does require some practice. And as long as the bowl is made of porcelain, it is not too difficult to balance it in one's hand even when it is filled with steaming rice. But it is a very different matter if the bowl is made of silver or any other metal. Since metal conducts heat rapidly, eating out of a silver bowl containing steaming hot rice can be a most unpleasant experience. For this reason, it is unusual to find silver rice bowls even in the homes of the most extravagant peranakan businessmen.

As for the kinds of utensils used in serving tea and coffee, it is true that the wealthy and more anglicized babas who regularly invited their English and European friends to their magnificent homes, served tea and coffee out of expensive sterling silver utensils imported either from Britain or France. But these were exceptions to the normal practice in most peranakan households throughout the Straits Settlements. Indeed, judging by the quantity of pretty antique porcelain teapots and teacups which have been recovered from old Straits Chinese homes, it appears that tea-drinking in Chinese style must have been a very popular pastime. Tea preparation, however, is an ancient art which requires, among other things, the know-how of seasoning a teapot, the art of selecting different grades of tea-leaves according to their special bouquet and the method of brewing the beverage to ensure freshness of taste. While there is clear evidence to show that tea was the universal beverage of every baba home, I have not been able to discover evidence of widespread tea connoisseurship among the peranakan Chinese.

Thus those splendid dinner, tea and coffee services made of sterling silver which were so highly prized in England and Europe as upper-class luxuries did not really appeal to the peranakan Chinese, accustomed as they had always been to the use of porcelain wares for all their household utensils. They preferred to lavish their appreciation on silver and gold jewellery and objects of *virtu*, which explains why most extant pieces of antique Straits silverwork tended to be small, jewel-like and intricately ornamented – the better pieces being particularly distinguished by their refinement of craftsmanship.

However, attempts to appreciate antique Straits Chinese silverwork do sometimes run into a snag, as we have noted previously. Westerners who are unfamiliar with the symbolism and religious iconography of ancient China may find the decorative designs of Straits silverwork disconcertingly grotesque, especially with regard to those figures of Taoist immortals. Likewise, the crowded and apparently chaotic manner with which the various decorative designs are juxtaposed against one another seems to indicate a disregard by Chinese silversmiths for aesthetic criteria of elegance in form and content. Nevertheless this initial feeling of chaotic complexity in Straits silverwork should wear off as one becomes more and more familiar with the style of the decorative patterns. A careful inspection of these pieces of silverwork would soon reveal that the 'bizarre birds and beasts' are in fact phoenixes, dragons and *ch'i-lings* (the Buddhist lion or Chinese unicorn). In addition to these mythical but auspicious animals, traditional

Chinese craftsmen might also add, from time to time, other auspicious animal motifs such as fishes, crabs, prawns, bats, squirrels, as well as insects of varous sorts. Then, too, one occasionally finds, interspersed among the animal motifs, Taoist and Buddhist symbols such as 'the eight baskets of blessing'. Floral and foliated designs should not present any difficulty as they are often realistically represented in terms of chrysanthemums, lotuses, plum blossoms and peonies.

Now this Chinese habit of juxtaposing a heterogeneous assortment of aesthetically unrelated symbols and motifs in an apparently disorganized fashion did in fact strike most early English writers and students of Malayan arts and crafts as hideous and outlandish. In direct contrast, Malay silverwork is a study in unified simplicity of design, clarity of expression and quiet elegance. Antique Malay silverwork is never encumbered by pictorial parables, religious and auspicious emblems, mythological figures and fantastic beasts, all intermingled in complex and mystical relations. For by the precepts of Islam, the Malay silversmith was strictly forbidden to incorporate any form of animal or anthropomorphic symbols in his decorative designs. Idolatry was taboo. He was, therefore, constrained to express his artistic inspirations in purely geometric or conventional floral and foliated motifs. The nett result is that all his works are pervaded with that characteristic sense of restrained and uncluttered beauty (see fig. 24). Thus, however intricate the ornamental designs of a piece of old Malay silver may be, the theme always com-

Fig. 24 A pair of silvergilt curtain hooks with impressive stem-plates ornamented entirely in floral and foliated motifs after the manner of arabesque work – unmistakably a product of Malay craftsmanship. Length of stem-plate: 20 cm. From Singapore. Mrs. Ho Wing Meng.

prises a combination of geometric patterns and conventional floral or foliated motifs delineated in an expressive style. If the teachings of Islam restricted artistic expression to the monotonous representation of arabesque designs in different variations, they also enabled Malay silversmiths to make a virtue of necessity, namely, the single-minded devotion to the creation of aesthetic designs, free from intrusions of all sorts of an-thropomorphic, zoomorphic and botanical motifs. In traditional Chinese art, however, ar-tistic licence sometimes played havoc with the requirements of aesthetic appeal.

Chinese art symbols, on the other hand, were rarely, if ever, intended to have purely orna-mental effects. For the Chinese have always been such a practical people that it is hard to imagine them rigidly espousing the principle of Art for Art's sake, even when they were turning out what would generally be regarded elsewhere

as objects of personal adornment. On the con-trary, whenever one finds a piece of old silver-work with certain specific types of human, animal or botanical motifs worked into the design, one can determine the ceremonial func-tion which the article in question served, by simply noting the kinds of symbols and motifs found on the artefact. For example, personal ornaments intended for wedding ceremonies will invariably be found to contain only those symbols which denote marital bliss (peonies and phoenixes), conjugal fidelity (a pair of mandarin ducks) and many male children (pomegranates with the seeds exposed, or perhaps, a pair of quails). Similarly, any article intended specifi-cally for birthday celebrations of important or elderly people should include those symbols which denote longevity (the Chinese character 寿, a peach, a stork, or an antelope), good luck (the character 福 and the bat) and prosperity (the figure of a pot-bellied mandarin scholar or a *ch'i-ling*).

In ancient China, too, the ornamental work found on pieces of utensils might be used to indicate the official rank or status of the person who happened to use or own the article in question. Thus the five-clawed dragon was traditionally reserved for use on the emperor's robes, seals, porcelain wares, jades and other royal insignia, while a pair of phoenixes was reserved for the use of the empress. Now the dragon is commonly found in Straits Chinese silverwork, except that it is usually depicted as a four-clawed saurian rather than a five-clawed one. Another common type of motif found in Straits silver is the set of three symbols representing the *San Twoh* (三多) or Three Abundances, namely, an old, bearded man holding a large, gnarled wooden rod and flanked on either side by a stork and an antelope (representing longevity), a lady carrying a baby in her arms (representing many children) and a pot-bellied mandarin scholar holding a *ju-i* sceptre (representing riches and success). The presentation of any silver article (e.g., one of those impressive buckles) bearing the symbols of The Abundances may be interpreted as an appropriate way of wishing the person concerned long life, many sons, riches and prosperity.

Sometimes a piece of Straits silver may include among its decorative motifs the symbols of a lute, a chess board, a pair of books and a pair of scrolls, depicted in a conventional rather than realistic fashion. These emblems signify the four scholarly accomplishments. Butterflies denote conjugal happiness and are frequently seen in objects or articles intended for the nonyas. The *ch'i-ling*, for all its monstrous and formidable appearance (having the head of a ferocious dragon with one horn, the body of a stag, the hoofs of a horse and the tail of an ox!) is, according to the legends of China, a gentle and benevolent creature. It was said to have appeared when Confucius was born! Hence, for over two millenia it came to be regarded as a symbol of wisdom, justice, success and good fortune. The mercantile and trading class among the Straits Chinese community were particularly fond of this motif.

The dragon is traditionally regarded in Western mythology as a symbol of everything that was evil. In Chinese folklore, however, this mythical saurian, whether of the winged, wingless, bald-headed or long-haired variety, was a symbol of everything that was great, awesome and auspicious. According to the records of the T'ang Dynasty (A.D. 618–906), it was the Empress Wu Tze-tien (武则天) who inaugurated the practice of using the emblem of a coiled dragon embroidered on official robes for presentation to deserving officials of her imperial court.[24] But it was not until the year A.D. 1111 that a royal edict from the court of Emperor Hui Tsung (徽宗) of the Southern Sung Dynasty (960–1279) made it illegal for any person who was not an official of the court nor a member of the royal family, to wear robes or other ceremonial costumes embroidered with dragon patterns. From then on, until about the end of the eighteenth century, the use of dragon motifs to decorate all artefacts and objects of art or *virtu* was strictly reserved for the regalia and insignia of the royal family and other high-born nobility. However, with the decline of the Ch'ing Dynasty after the death of the Emperor Ch'ien Lung in 1795, it became increasingly difficult to enforce the authority of the court in Peking, and the dragon motif soon became the commonest art symbol, embellishing even the humblest of daily utensils.

Since the symbolic significance of the decorative motifs takes priority over other aesthetic considerations, the Chinese craftsman was free to draw his artistic inspiration from the pantheistic and hospitable system of religious beliefs and folklore, an enormous and varied repertoire of art and religious motifs. They include at least a dozen species of flowering plants and fruit trees, at least a score of zoological species drawn from insects, birds, fishes, shells, crustacea and mammals; and if these proved to be inadequate, there was a generous supply of extraordinary beasts and beings culled from ancient mythologies to enrich his art work. If anything, the Chinese goldsmith and silversmith was never constrained by the precepts of his religious beliefs to express his sense of beauty in terms of a restricted category of conventional floral and foliated patterns. Nonetheless this artistic licence was restricted to the occasion or purpose for which a particular article was intended to be used. For example, an object intended for religious offerings on All Saints' Day would not normally include in its ornamental design all those motifs which are appropriate for birthday celebrations or, for

that matter, those motifs fit for marriage ceremonies.

General characteristics

We may now sum up with a few remarks about the general characteristics of Straits Chinese silverwork. Although practically all extant pieces of Straits silver may be attributed to the handiwork of Chinese silversmiths trained in the tradition of gold and silver craftsmanship in ancient China, the shapes and functions of most of these artefacts made to Straits Chinese specifications were non-Chinese in inspiration. This, as we have previously noted, may be attributed to the Malayan influence in Straits Chinese culture. However, in fabricating all those articles intended for the Straits nonyas, Straits silversmiths did not slavishly imitate Malay-Sumatran or Malay-Javanese silverwork but modified and adapted them to suit local tastes. This is shown by the fact that the decorative motifs of most extant pieces of Straits silverwork were entirely drawn from traditional Chinese art and religious symbols rather than the standard arabesque patterns of flowers and twining foliage so commonly seen in the art of Islam.

The same applies to the style of interpreting Chinese motifs in the decorative designs of these artefacts. Instead of expressing their decorative work in terms of simple arabesque of twining foliated patterns after the manner of Malay silverwares, the Straits silversmith tended to employ a heterogeneous collection of aesthetically unrelated, but symbolically significant symbols to enhance the ornamental work of a piece of silver artefact. Moreover, these motifs are interpreted so ornately that anyone encountering samples of Straits silverwork for the first time will be struck by the sense of dazzling complexity which these artefacts present. And unless one is able to recognize the symbolic and auspicious nature of the various symbols employed and the manner in which they are arranged, the decorative designs of these silverwork will appear to be more complicated and bizarre. After this initial reaction, one realizes that the overall conception of the decorative design is often recognizably clear and simple. One simply needs to familiarize oneself with the presence of these bizarre-looking motifs and understand the iconography of these symbols. When, with a little practice, one is able to 'decipher' the meanings of the various symbols, and when one has learnt to notice how the various motifs are arranged within the decorative design, so that they reinforce one another in expressing some auspicious theme or message, the feeling of perplexity disappears altogether. For one does not 'see' how the composition of a work of art 'hangs' together until one has understood the meanings, and the functions, of all the other elements which go into the making of the theme.

Still, when all is said and done, the fact remains that Straits Chinese silverwork does, in fact, present a picture of ornate complexity. Such was the characteristic style of eighteenth/nineteenth-century Chinese art and craftsmanship. From a historical point of view, the evolution of this manner of ornamenting silverwork could be attributed to the prevailing tastes of imperial patrons (from the time of the Emperor Ch'ien Lung [1736–95] down to the end of the Ch'ing Dynasty) for ornate designs executed in repoussé or high relief work, rather than the low-keyed chased work and simple engravings of the earlier period pieces dating back to the T'ang Dynasty. As every student of silverwork knows, the repoussé technique of raising the details of the ornamental work well above the surface of a piece of metal, when employed exclusively, tends to give a three-dimensional appearance to each of the decorative motifs. However, when the various motifs employed happen to belong to different categories of objects, and they are crowded together, the nett effect of combining these different sorts of patterns within the restricted space of a relatively small piece of silver article (and Straits silver articles are usually small), is to give the impression of an over-encrusted object rather than an aesthetically uncluttered object.

In fact, the common criticism directed against Straits silverwork was that the overwrought designs of most extant pieces tended to lower, rather than enhance, the attractiveness of Chinese craftsmanship. Malay workmanship, by contrast, was elegantly simple. That may well be so, except that in the eyes of their devotees,

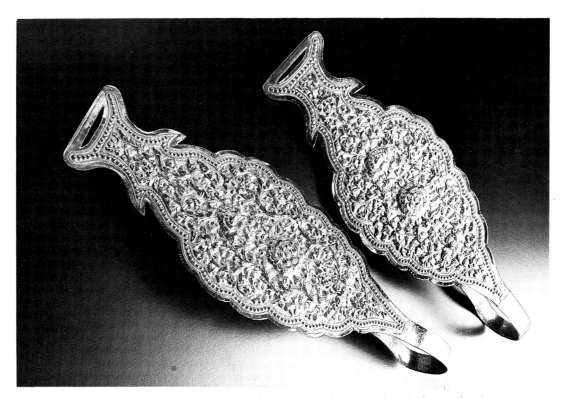

Fig. 25 A pair of curtain hooks made to Malay taste. The ogival stem-plate is ornamented with peony blossoms and twining foliage depicted in characteristic arabesque style. This pair of curtain hooks is not of Malay, but rather Straits Chinese craftsmanship – the tell-tale clue being the realistic depiction of the peony blossoms. Malay floral motifs are always abstract and formalized. Length: 24 cm. From Singapore.

Fig. 26 This delightful-looking plate, with a flat rim of purely floral and foliated motifs, closely resembles one of those old Malay dishes shown in Roth's *Oriental Silverwork*. But it is obviously a product of local Chinese silversmiths, judging by the crisp and clearly identifiable prunus blossoms executed in pierced work. Diameter: 12 cm. From Singapore.

such strictures against Straits Chinese decorative arts appeared to cut no ice at all. Quite the contrary. These artefacts were the relics of a unique cultural heritage – and that was what matters most. The aesthetics of Straits Chinese craftmanship was a separate issue, and taste was not something fixed once and for all time. If there is one thing about which art critics are unanimous in holding, it is the notorious fact about the variability of tastes. Besides, the finer pieces of Straits silverwork need no apology.

Apart from that, there was never any doubt at all in the minds of most people that Straits silversmiths in the days gone by were perfectly capable of producing convincing imitations of the typical arabesque designs of Malay silverwork. Examples of extant pieces executed in this style (see figs. 25 & 26) are proofs of their skills. Nonetheless, the monotony of having to operate with a very restricted number of art motifs certainly did not appeal to them. For one thing, it was inconsistent with the spirit of Chinese art to employ decorative motifs only for the purpose of beautifying the surface of an arti-

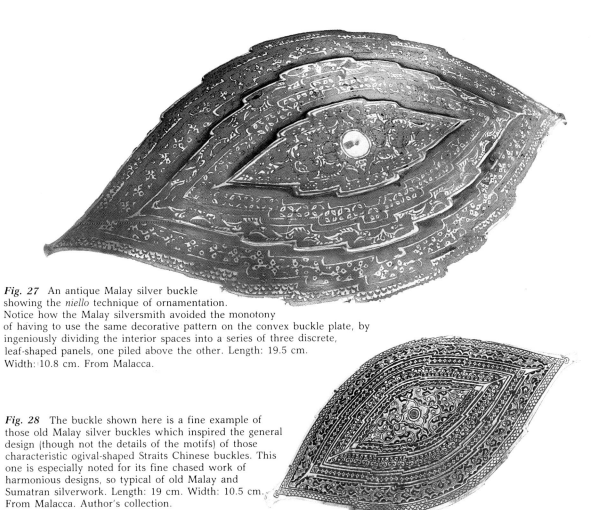

Fig. 27 An antique Malay silver buckle showing the *niello* technique of ornamentation. Notice how the Malay silversmith avoided the monotony of having to use the same decorative pattern on the convex buckle plate, by ingeniously dividing the interior spaces into a series of three discrete, leaf-shaped panels, one piled above the other. Length: 19.5 cm. Width: 10.8 cm. From Malacca.

Fig. 28 The buckle shown here is a fine example of those old Malay silver buckles which inspired the general design (though not the details of the motifs) of those characteristic ogival-shaped Straits Chinese buckles. This one is especially noted for its fine chased work of harmonious designs, so typical of old Malay and Sumatran silverwork. Length: 19 cm. Width: 10.5 cm. From Malacca. Author's collection.

cle. For another, it was technically stifling to be constrained to express one's artistic skills in terms of a few standardized type of decorative patterns. And notwithstanding the idiosyncracies of some patrons and the constraints imposed by the tradition of his profession, every craftsman worth his salt would welcome every opportunity to express the full potentialities of his skills. Indeed one has only to examine extant pieces of Straits silverwork in order to appreciate the range of his technical competence in applying such standard techniques as repoussé work, chased work, engraving, pierced work, appliqué work, filigree work, granulation work, box-setting, *à jour* setting, and gilding by cold-press, mercury gilding and chemical-electro plating, to depict the extensive varieties of anthropomorphic, zoomorphic and botanical motifs intrinsic to Straits silverwork.

Although practically all the known techniques of crafting gold and silverwork are found in extant pieces of Straits silverwork, the techniques of repoussé and chased work are by far the most popular methods employed in depicting the decorative designs. Engraving and filigree work, however, are infrequently used. For some reason or other, these techniques of crafting precious metals appeared to have been more widely accepted in China than in the Straits Settlements. The same is true of the appliqué technique which is rarely seen in Straits silverwork. There is one popular Malay-Sumatran technique which Straits silversmiths never tried to emulate, and that is *niello* work (see figs. 27 & 28). *Niello* work is the technique of filling all the depressed spaces between the chased designs with a bluish-black substance or enamel, and then polishing the surface until the decorative patterns emerge against the contrasting background of bluish-black.

Finally, the fact that Straits silver was fundamentally the product of the fusion of two different cultural traditions, namely, Hindu-Islamic and Chinese, has, in my opinion, redounded to the advantage of the Chinese silversmith. Among other things, the need to express the best in the two styles of craftsmanship somehow prevented Straits Chinese silverwork from degenerating into gimcracks loaded with a mass of superfluous ornamental protuberances and encrustations that one finds, for example, in the more baroque pieces of French and German silverwork. It is true that the prevailing tastes of eighteenth/nineteenth-century Chinese silverwork demanded a more elaborate and crowded style of decoration than was fashionable in earlier period silverwares going back to the T'ang Dynasty. But even here, it is instructive to note that the Straits silversmith never lost his sense of good taste: the most ornate designs of Straits silverwork were never allowed to be so obtrusively conspicuous as to interfere with the symmetry or organic wholeness of the object in question. For example, a teapot or wine ewer, whatever its ornamental design may take, is always and immediately recognizable as such.

Straits Chinese gold

Extant examples of Straits Chinese gold are few and far between. Most of them are family heirlooms handed down over several generations and are now greatly treasured, partly for their superb craftsmanship, and partly for the eternal fascination which gold exercises upon the imagination of most people. Students of Straits Chinese material culture, however, rarely have the opportunity of seeing them, because they are jealously guarded and salted away in bank vaults most of the time. Indeed, I have seen no more than ten such pieces of old Straits Chinese gold in the course of the last twelve years or so. There are, of course, no lack of contemporary Chinese gold ornaments and jewellery in modern-day goldsmiths throughout Singapore and Malaysia, but collectors of antique gold made to Straits Chinese taste will look in vain for these artefacts in goldsmith shops.

Since these articles are of such great variety (but they were not all that rare during the late nineteenth and early twentieth century) what, one wonders, do they really look like? In fig. 30 we illustrate several representative specimens of antique Straits Chinese gold which came from Singapore, Malacca and Penang; and it will be noticed at once that as far as the shapes of these artefacts, the kind of ornamental motifs they sport and characteristic style of workmanship are concerned, they are so very similar to Straits silver that they could have been mistaken for *silverwork*, were it not for the presence of stamped marks proclaiming the base metal to be gold. The close similarity between Straits Chinese gold and silver is not really surprising when we remember that the craftsmen who fabricated the great bulk of old Straits silver-

Fig. 29 Gold ornaments of antique workmanship such as this lovely belt and matching buckle, executed entirely in fine pierced work, are very rarely encountered nowadays. This is an example of superb craftsmanship dating back to about the turn of the present century. The gold is 18-carat and thus sufficiently hard for the fabricating of a belt. From Penang. Mariette collection.

Fig. 30 There are easily over one hundred goldsmiths operating in Singapore and the various towns of West Malaysia today. But the student of Straits silver will look in vain for antique gold ornaments of the types shown in this picture. The large ogival-shaped buckle, done in repoussé work, is an example of the superb craftsmanship practised by goldsmiths and silversmiths of that bygone era during the nineteenth century. From various parts of Malaysia. Mariette collection.

work also worked in gold, as and when they received special orders from their wealthy clients for specific objects to be fashioned out of gold. It is true that most of their handiwork were in silver or silvergilt. This is because the bullion value of silver was so much lower than that of gold. Besides, the shrewd Chinese silversmith had sufficient business acumen to realise that the only way in which he could cater to a larger clientele was to turn out more silver artefacts than those made of gold. Since silver could easily be made to simulate the feel and appearance of gold by a thin veneer of

gilding for a small premium, the profit-conscious silversmith needed no further persuasion as to where his priority lay.

Be that as it may, the fact remains that the wealthier baba clients, whose fondness for ostentation was proverbial, insisted that those articles intended for ceremonial purposes as well as for personal ornaments, including jewellery, should be fabricated in real gold. Silvergilt was just not good enough. As for the local silversmith, he was only too eager to oblige, because important commissions to fabricate articles of gold always provided the right sort of opportuni-

Fig. 31 This is one of the finest Straits Chinese buckles that I have seen in all these years. The sheer exuberance and precision of the repoussé motifs make this article rank among the best of Straits silverwork. The craftsman who fabricated this jewel of a buckle must have derived considerable satisfaction in contemplating his own handiwork. Silver-gilt. Length: 15.5 cm. Width: 11.5 cm. From Singapore. Author's collection.

ties to demonstrate his craftsmanship to the fullest, and enabled him to further establish his reputation with other well-to-do peranakan clients. For it must be remembered that in the days before the advent of mass communication and mass media, the fame of a goldsmith or silversmith was spread by word of mouth. Satisfied customers provided the most effective form of advertisement.

As far as Straits Chinese gold and silver are concerned, there is practically little or no difference, from a stylistic point of view, between a finely crafted piece of silverwork and its counterpart in gold. If the silver artefact is gilded, the distinction is even harder to make out. Thus the silvergilt buckle in fig. 31 is to all intents and purposes indistinguishable from the gold buckle shown in fig. 30. On the whole, Straits Chinese gold ornaments tended to be crafted with greater care and refinement. Higher cost is probably an important factor in determining the quality of workmanship. The belt and buckle set shown in fig. 29 sporting formalized butterfly panels and an ogival-shaped buckle executed in pierced work, is a lovely example of Straits Chinese gold at its best.

4 The Various Categories of Straits Chinese Silver

N OW THAT THE general characteristics of Straits silverwork have been outlined in the previous chapter, we may proceed to discuss in greater detail the special features of each of the various categories of Straits silver artefacts which had somehow survived the vicissitudes of time and the fiery crucible of the smelter's furnace. At least seventeen different types of artefacts in extant have been selected here for analysis, both with regard to their special functions and their stylistic peculiarities. Some of the pieces illustrated in this book are not of Straits Chinese origin but rather of South China or Malay-Sumatran origins. They have been included here mainly to enable the student of Straits silver to compare and differentiate the salient features of local Chinese silver from those of other provenance. Naturally, one cannot hope to acquire real expertise by simply studying the illustrations (no matter how good they are) in the book. But it is to be hoped that these pictures and their accompanying descriptions in the text will provide a pretext for further inquiry.

I should also like to note, in passing, that the task of finding representative samples of each and every extant type of Straits silverwork had not been an easy one when I first started out to write this work. This is because most of the museums in Malaysia and Singapore did not, until very recently, possess more than just a few token and nondescript pieces. As for private collections of Straits silver, these were practically non-existent until the provenance and attribution of these artefacts had been established. I am pleased to note that the publication of my book has greatly stimulated students' and collectors' interest in this hitherto unknown and neglected heritage of the traditional peranakan Chinese community. Even the major museums in Malaysia and Singapore have now taken cognizance of Straits Chinese silver by acquiring representative samples in their collections. There are not many private collections of Straits silver in Malaysia and Singapore, and the few that I have had the privilege of studying have only been built up in recent years. All in all, the student of Straits silver today would have an easier task than I did some ten years ago.

Buntal plates

It was customary for the peranakan Chinese, in the days gone by, to attach specially crafted pieces of silver plates to the opposite ends of pillows and bolsters intended for the bridal bed. This was a practice which the traditional Straits Chinese borrowed from the natives of Malacca. The custom was not indigenous to China, for pillow and bolster plates were never used in ancient China. Such pillow and bolster plates, known as *buntal*

Fig. 32 This octagonal bolster plate (one of a pair), with its formalized floral and foliated motifs executed in repoussé work, is a typical example of old Malay silverwork. Longest width: 14 cm. From Penang.

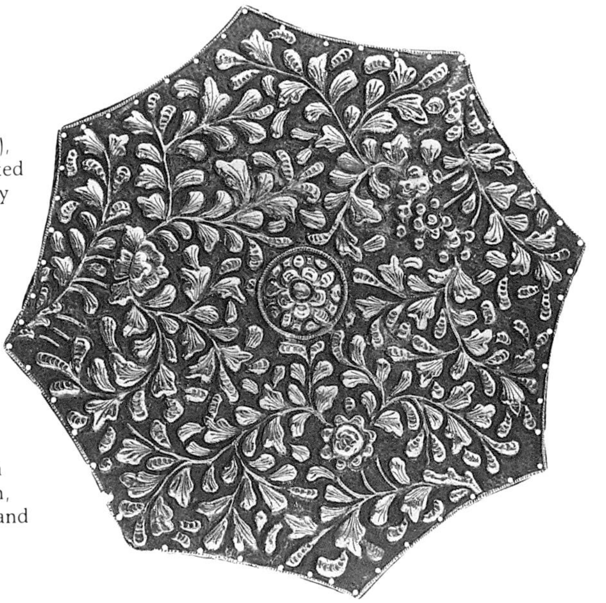

Fig. 33 This pillow plate (buntal kepala), one of a pair, is of typical Malay craftsmanship. The design, confined to the depiction of highly stylized floral and foliated motifs, is expressed in the characteristic arabesque style and executed in repoussé work. Length: 18.5 cm. Width: 8 cm. From Johore.

kepala and buntal pelok respectively, are among the most commonly encountered samples of Straits silverwork, and most of the older generations of nonyas in Penang, Malacca and Singapore usually treasure a few pairs of these buntal plates among the various bric-à-brac of family heirlooms.

Generally speaking, there are two types of buntal plates, one for pillow ends and the other for bolster ends; and they usually come in pairs. Since buntal plates had also been regularly used by upper-class Malays and their royalty, students of Straits silver may have some difficulty distinguishing between Chinese buntal plates and those of Malay origin. For these people the following pointers may be useful.

Size for size, Chinese silver plate is thicker and heavier than Malay silver plate. But on the whole, Straits Chinese buntal plates are smaller and less ostentatious than the large and impressive pieces made for huge ceremonial bolsters and pillows of Malay royalty. Incidentally, those huge, box-like pillows ornamented on either ends with impressive buntal kepala and fat, barrel-like 'Dutch-wives', resplendent in brocade and glittering buntal pelok as seen in pictures of Malay royal weddings, were more ceremonial than utilitarian. Among the Straits Chinese varieties of buntal plates, the pillow ends are always rectangular in shape and their dimensions vary between 11 cm and 15 cm in length and 6.5 cm and 9 cm in width. Bolster ends (buntal pelok), on the other hand, come in two different shapes, (1) the circular pieces measuring, on the average, between 10.5

Fig. 34 In this pillow plate, one of a pair, the Malay silversmith has arranged his simple arabesque scrolls in such a way that they 'flow' as it were, in a continuous movement, around the central rectangular panel. This feel for harmony and simplicity of design is one of the most attractive features of Malay workmanship. Length: 17.5 cm. Width: 8 cm. From Johore.

Fig. 35 The beauty of this typically Malay *buntal* plate (one of a pair) lies in the skill with which the simple and uncluttered design of the decorative motifs is depicted. As with most of Islamic floral motifs, it is not easy to say what species of 'flowers the floral spray depicted here belongs to: it bears some resemblance to peony blossoms. Notice how clearly the various components of the floral sprays are articulated. Originally gilded, but only light traces of gilding remain. Length: 18.8 cm. Width: 8.8 cm. From Malacca.

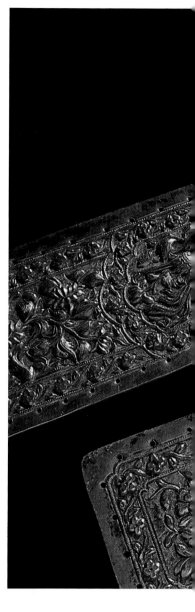

cm in diameter, and (2) the octagonal pieces with a width of approximately 11 cm.

Malay *buntal* plates (see figs. 32–35) do not, however, come in more or less standard sizes typical of the Straits Chinese varieties: they varied with the wealth and social status of the person or family who commissioned them. The smaller and commoner types of Malay *buntal* plates are about the same dimensions as those used by the Straits babas; but the larger ones (probably intended for the rajahs and sultans) may be anything up to 20 cm in diameter for *buntal pelok*, and 30 cm by 20 cm for the *buntal kepala*.

As for the *buntal* plates intended for the Straits babas, since there were no class or social distinctions based on hereditary nobility or royalty (the peranakans being a predominantly merchant-trading community) there was no necessity to brand-

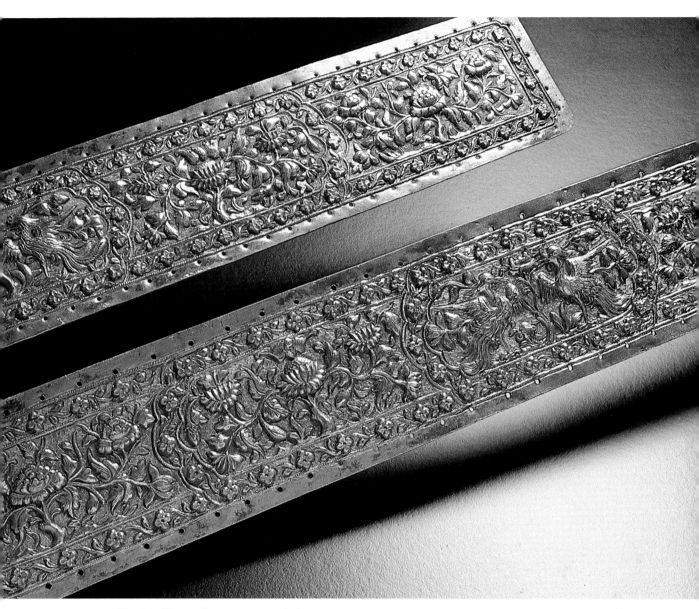

Fig. 36 The two long, ornamented silver panels shown here are not pillow plates of the type traditionally made for Straits Chinese families. They were probably made for the use of the Malay nobility (note the exclusive use of birds and floral motifs), and they must have been used for decorating the sides of some ceremonial cushion made of velvet and stuffed with cotton wool. There should be two other shorter panels. Length: 30 cm. Mariette collection.

ish one's social status by the sizes of the *buntal* plates used for wedding ceremonies. But the wealthier baba families did, however, commission *buntal* plates of heavily gilded silver (and even gold!) ornamented with exquisite motifs of refined workmanship.

Apart from the fact that Malay *buntal* plates differ from those of the Straits babas in their overall dimensions, their decorative designs, in accordance with the precepts of Islam, consisted exclusively of formalized floral and foliated motifs arranged in arabesque patterns. The decorative designs of the Straits Chinese types of *buntal* plates, however, adhered to the traditional Chinese style of employing a heterogeneous collection of mythical and propitious symbols with phoenixes, peonies and butterflies recurring frequently.

Fig. 37 Three representative samples of pillow plates in silvergilt made for Straits
Chinese clients. The decorative designs are all done in repoussé work, but the quality of
the workmanship is not the same. The *buntal* plate on the left is a typical example of
what I call 'Johore work', while the plates on the right come from Malacca. The top
buntal plate (one of a pair) is said to have come from the heirloom of a wealthy family.
Average length: 16 cm. Width: 10 cm. Author's collection.

Pillow ends

Generally speaking, the ornamental designs of *pillow* ends are separated into two principal compartments, namely, a central rectangular panel enclosed by a broad rectangular border. Since the traditional practice of the decorative arts in China required that auspicious symbols of the appropriate sorts be incorporated into the decorative design, the only way of satisfactorily meeting this requirement without producing an impression of chaotic complexity was to put different types of motifs in different panels, each having clearly demarcated boundaries (see figs. 37 & 38). Unfortunately, this precept was not always strictly adhered to, with the result that many extant pieces of *buntal* plates (see figs. 39 & 40) present an exasperatingly cluttered and disorganized appearance.

Fig. 38 This pair of finely crafted pillow plates is in the best of Straits Chinese taste. Notice that the ornamental motifs are clearly articulated and well spaced out so as not to give that cluttered appearance which impairs the aesthetic value of those commoner pieces of Straits silverwork. Silvergilt. Length: 16 cm. Width: 10.5 cm. From Malacca. Author's collection.

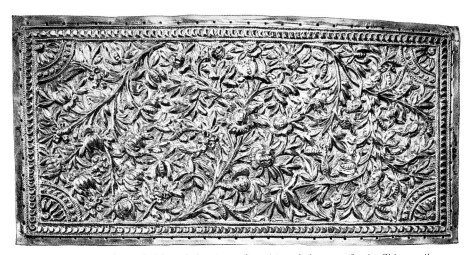

Fig. 39 This Malay-styled *buntal* plate (one of a pair) made by some Straits Chinese silversmith was obviously intended for some Malay clients, otherwise there was no reason for confining the decorative design to purely floral and foliated motifs. However, in his anxiety to conform to Islamic taste, the silversmith went to the other extreme of loading the decorative design with a plethora of what looks like the flowers of the four seasons arranged in higgledy-piggledy fashion. If anything, this *buntal* plate is a paradigm case of what ought not to be done to a piece of silverwork. Length 18.8 cm. Width: 9.2 cm. From Johore.

Fig. 40 Octagonal bolster end (one of a pair) showing a rather cluttered appearance. The central circular medallion depicts a *ch'i-ling*, while the outer panel reveals, on closer inspection, the flowers of the four seasons positioned along the four cardinal points of the compass, two scholars' emblems and two Taoist emblems. The higgledy-piggledy look of this *buntal* plate is largely due to the failure to emphasize the principal motifs sufficiently by toning down the leaves and all the other string-like appendages. Silvergilt. From Singapore.

For all their obsessive preoccupation with the symbolic meanings of art motifs, Straits silversmiths did recognize the need to preserve a sense of organic unity within the complex of heterogeneous symbols which constitute the contents of their decorative designs. This is clearly indicated by the fact that even among those extant pieces of *buntal* plates in which the different motifs have not been partitioned off by discrete panels or boundary lines, the Chinese silversmith made efforts to restore some semblance of organization by positioning those motifs belonging to some common theme (e.g., the flowers of the four seasons) along the four cardinal points of the compass. The intervening spaces are then filled up with another set of motifs belonging to a different set of auspicious symbols (see figs. 41 & 42).

Fig. 41 There is something about the style of workmanship peculiar to this pair of bolster plates, especially the characteristic vigour and boldness of the motifs and that unmistakable border design of simple rings, which suggests that this pair of *buntal* plates was probably made by the same hands which crafted the bolster plates shown in figs. 32 and 44. Notice the unusual pose of the phoenix in the central medallion. Diameter: 12 cm. From Singapore. Author's collection.

Fig. 42 There is a sense of vigour and movement about the ornamental motifs of this remarkable pair of bolster plates. The presence of the pair of phoenixes and peony blossoms clearly indicate that these *buntal* plates were intended for the bridal bolsters. Silvergilt. Diameter: 10.5 cm. From Singapore. Author's collection.

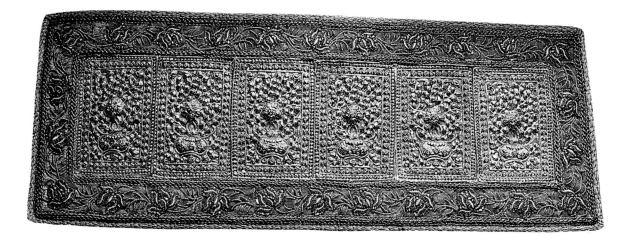

Fig. 43 This unusual rectangular panel of felt and cotton fabrics mounted with six small pieces of silver plates ornamented with flower-basket motifs, comes from an old Penang home. It is said to be an ornamental wrap for securing together the embroidered curtains of a bridal bed. It is unique to Penang. Length: 25 cm. Width: 12 cm. Mrs. Ho Wing Meng.

The ornamental motifs of most *buntal* plates consist mostly of chased and relief work, but from time to time one encounters some pieces executed with a combination of pierced and relief work. A combination of pierced and relief work was probably harder to execute because Chinese silver plate tended to be thicker than Malay silver plate and thus much harder to perforate even with sharp punches. No examples of filigree work or appliqué work have been encountered in Straits *buntal* plates, probably because such techniques of silverwork did not appeal to the Straits babas.

Quality of workmanship is generally of a high standard though there are undoubtedly pieces of shoddy quality. Among the better pieces, the ornamental details are often rendered with a sense of realism which is further enhanced by clear-cut reliefs to give the impression of carving in the round. The types of symbols which feature predominantly in *buntal* plates are *ch'i-lings* (usually positioned in the central panel), the flowers of the four seasons usually interspersed with two or four emblems of the Taoist immortals, peonies and phoenixes. The most commonly employed symbols of Taoism are (1) a fan with a fly-whisk which was the emblem of Han Chung-li

(韩仲尼), the chief of the immortals, and (2) the pilgrim gourd, the emblem of Li Tien-kuai (李田侩) who is always represented as an emaciated beggar holding a crutch in one hand and a gourd in the other.

By and large, Straits silversmiths did not always adhere to the conventional practice of incorporating into their decorative designs the full complement of any of these sets of symbols. They preferred to select no more than half or a quarter of the total number of symbols from some propitious theme and combine them with a similar proportion of motifs culled from another theme. For example, the emblems of Taoist immortals are frequently complemented with those denoting scholarly accomplishments. Although the presence of such auspicious symbols in the decorative designs of Straits silverwork was clearly intended to express good wishes or congratulatory messages at weddings, birthdays or anniversaries, it is doubtful whether the great majority of traditional babas in Malacca, Penang and Singapore understood their meanings or purposes. Still they faithfully observed all the rites and rituals of their community because tradition prescribed such ancient practices.

Fig. 44 A pair of octagonal bolster plates in typical Straits Chinese style. Notice that the motifs, executed in repoussé work, and consisting of a fat *ch'i-ling* in the central medallion, two magpie-like birds, a bat and peony blossoms in the surrounding panels, are depicted in a bold and vigorous fashion. Repoussé work. Largest width: 11.5 cm. From Singapore.

Bolster ends

As befitting the objects for which they were to adorn, bolster ends or *buntal pelok* (see figs. 44–46) always come in pairs. But they are of two different shapes: circular and octagonal. Square or hexagonal plates have never been encountered. Superficially, the appearance of the circular type of *buntal pelok* reminds one of the backs of those early bronze mirrors dating from the Han to the T'ang Dynasty, except that the ornamental designs of Straits *buntal* plates are far more crowded than the designs of T'ang period mirror backs. Like pillow ends, the baba type of bolster plates are generally smaller than those of Malay origin – the diameter of the average plate measures no more than 10 cm. It is possible, though no independent evidence is yet available, that the older variety of Straits *buntal* plates (i.e., those dating to the late eighteenth or early nineteenth

century) were more lightly and evenly gilded and came in thinner plates. As with pillow plates, too, the quality (and correspondingly the price) of any piece of bolster end was determined by the standard and refinement of workmanship rather than the sheer size of the plate.

Generally, whether a *buntal* plate is circular or octagonal, the layout of the decorative motifs consists quite simply of a central, circular or octagonal panel enclosed by a broad, concentric border which carries the bulk of the ornamental work. The central panel invariably bears one single, dominant motif which could either be that of a *ch'i-ling*, a dragon, a phoenix or a stork. As for the broad border surrounding it, Straits silversmiths worked into it the conventional types of art and auspicious motifs including Taoist emblems, peonies, phoenixes and flowers of the four seasons. The treatment and interpretation of the motifs, however, vary from one craftsman to another.

Fig. 45 This octagonal bolster plate (one of a pair) with inward-curving sides is fabricated out of a rather thick sheet of silver plate. The motifs, depicting the flowers of the four seasons, are stiff and have a cluttered appearance. Silvergilt. Widest width: 11 cm. From Singapore.

Fig. 46 An unusual circular bolster plate. It is not often that such a profusion of assorted motifs including cockles, gastropods, mud crabs, king crabs (*Limnulus*), fishes (several species), seaweeds, flowers, scholarly symbols, monkeys and pine tree are thrown together willy-nilly in a *buntal* plate. But this one has them all! The overall effect is one of denseness but certainly not of utter chaos – mainly, one suspects, because the silversmith who crafted this *buntal* plate was skilful enough to modulate the various individual motifs in such a way that, while every object represented in the design was clearly articulated, some were emphasized while others were 'toned down' as it were. Mark of 'Ching Fu'. Diameter: 10 cm. From Singapore. Author's collection.

While Straits silverwork is noted for the ornateness of their ornamental work one occasionally encounters (see fig. 47) a piece executed with charming simplicity. The example shown in fig. 47 shows a *buntal* plate decorated quite unpretentiously with a rather fat-looking stork (in the central panel) standing on one leg amidst a background of sparse vegetation. A double circular ring clearly defines and isolates this central motif from the rest of the floral patterns in the surrounding, concentric band. The floral patterns consist of four simple sprays of lotuses and peonies (two of each species) arranged in a simple and symmetrical fashion: the two sprays of peonies are placed opposite each other in a north-south alignment, while the two sprays of lotuses are also placed opposite each other but in an east-west alignment. Their leaves and branches spread out to fill up the intervening spaces. Notice that the floral motifs are more conventional than realistic, but they are bold and expressively depicted. The gilding on this piece is of a light yellowish tinge and the plate is surprisingly thin. The thin outermost border is relatively unadorned except for a series of circular dots.

By contrast, the circular *buntal* plate in fig. 46 is a more complex piece of craftsmanship. The central circular panel depicts a pair of long-tailed gibbons, one of which is clinging to the trunk of an old pine tree. A thin, double-ring border chased with lattice-patterns encloses the central theme. It is in the broad circular band surrounding the central panel which displays an amazing assortment of aesthetically unrelated, but auspiciously significant motifs, lumped together in some higgledy-piggledy fashion. A closer inspection

Fig. 47 This is an unusual bolster-end plate (*buntal pelok*) executed in typical Straits Chinese taste. The neatness and bold simplicity of the design depicting the flowers of the four seasons and a fat stork in the central medallion, are obviously not in keeping with the typical nonya's taste for crowded and ornate designs. Notice that the narrow, outer border is simply ornamented with a series of circular rings. Silvergilt. Diameter: 11.5 cm. From Singapore.

reveals the presence of several species of fishes including carps and what looks like the Yellow River sturgeon, crabs of two types (one of which belongs to the Order of *Limnulus*), cockles, turbaned shells, seaweeds, plum blossoms, peonies, chrysanthemums and two emblems of scholarly accomplishments! If anything, the ornamental design of this *buntal* plate would appear to be a paradigm case of chaotic complexity in Straits Chinese silverwork.

And yet, for all its apparent sense of disorderliness, there is something rather attractive about the craftsmanship of this *buntal* plate. In particular, the sense of vigour, the sureness of touch and the realism of the carvings, all of which indicate that the silversmith who executed this plate was no fumbling tyro, but a skilled and experienced craftsman who obviously took a special delight in depicting the forms and appearances of marine animals. It says well of the craftsman that he was able to combine his knowledge of the special forms of marine animals with the technical fluency of his craftsmanship so effectively, that he practically transformed a plain piece of metal into an object of *virtu*.

If this *buntal* plate is reminiscent of fine craftsmanship in miniature, it is worth remembering that no extant pieces of Straits silverwork are large and showy after the fashion of those stupendous salvers characteristic of European silver. And the same is true of silverwares made in China, from T'ang Dynasty during the seventh century A.D. to the end of the nineteenth century. For even silverwares made for high-born nobility in China had always tended to be relatively small and unobtrusive. Contrary to hearsay, this preference for objects of *virtu* in silver was dictated not by financial stringency arising out of the high cost of silver bullion or, for that matter, the rarity of the metal. After all, the Chinese had regularly used 'saddle money' made out of silver ingots. Rather, the preference was influenced by a tradition of aesthetics which placed high premium on excellence of craftsmanship.

Buntal plates for neck rests?

The more observant among collectors of Straits silverwork may have noticed from time to time that there is a certain type of *buntal* plate which one encounters occasionally among the knick-knacks of an old silversmith in Johore and Malacca. These *buntal* plates are no longer than 10 cm long and 5 cm wide, and are ornamented with the usual peony blossoms, butterflies, phoenixes and auspicious Buddhist/Taoist symbols. When I first began to examine systematically the different types of Straits silverwork that were in extant some fourteen years ago, the presence of these somewhat diminutive pillow-end plates did not strike me as being particularly interesting or unusual, though I did note that they were less than half the size of the more standard types of *buntal kepala* plates measuring 15 cm long and 9 cm wide. However, I paid little or no attention to the *mere* size of any *buntal* plates, since it was a well-known fact that the sizes of *buntal* plates varied considerably, especially among those made for Malay clients. What I did not realize at the time

Fig. 48 This elegant pair of curtain hooks sports a distinctive stem-plate of beaten silver modified to look like a flower basket. The delicate, lace-like effect was largely achieved by the careful application of the pierced and repoussé techniques. Length of stem-plate: 10 cm. From Singapore.

was that *buntal* plates made for Straits Chinese clients, whether rich or of modest means, did *not* vary significantly in dimensions, but only in the *quality* of the workmanship. And these little *buntal* plates were, judging by their traditional Chinese motifs, intended for Straits Chinese clients. Why, then, were they significantly smaller?

The clue came to me several years later as I was casually flipping through the pages of Ling Roth's *Oriental Silverwork*. Fig.92 was a picture of one of these diminutive plates cryptically labelled 'Silver Plate for Chinese Neck Rest'. It occurred to me immediately that Roth was probably referring to one of those cubical-shaped porcelain or reddish lacquer pillows or head-rests which the older generations of Chinese women habitually used in the days gone by – my paternal grandmother regularly used one of those lacquer head-rests. Evidently Roth's description aptly fitted these little *buntal* plates.

The only snag about this assumption is that those cubical neck rests which Roth apparently

had in mind were by and large made of porcelain, stoneware, lacquer or some other hard and unyielding material; while these diminutive *buntal* plates were always equipped with needle holes along the edges to enable them to be sewn on to the sides of some more yielding pillow-like objects. All extant *buntal* plates were in fact made to be sewn on to the sides of pillows or the ends of bolsters which, naturally, had to be made of silk, velvet or cotton and stuffed with the cotton wool of the *kapok* tree.

It seems clear, therefore, that such *buntal* plates could not, as Roth alleged, have been made for Chinese neck rests of the types we commonly see in old Chinese homes. Apart from that, the baba-nonyas did not make use of such neck rests. It is more plausible to assume that these *buntal* plates were meant for *smaller* pillows made of fabric and stuffed with cotton wool, and that such pillows were meant for little children. But this is purely speculative, for I have yet to see such *buntal* plates *in situ*.

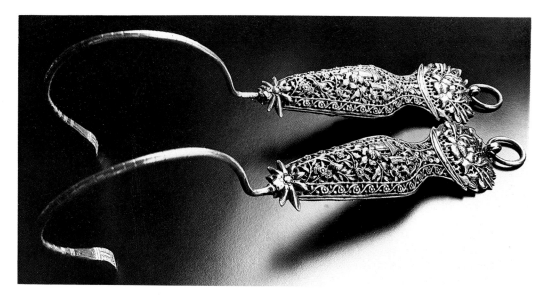

Fig. 49 In this pair of curtain hooks, the silversmith has ingeniously sought to design the stem-plates in such a way that they give the appearance of flower vases. The decorative motifs, consisting mainly of peonies and prunus blossoms, are crafted on both sides of the stem-plates, and are executed in pierced work. The workmanship is neat despite the ornateness of the decorative design. Length of stem-plate: 14 cm. From Singapore. Courtesy of Katong Antique House.

Curtain hooks

The traditional wedding bed of the peranakan Chinese in Singapore and Malaya was a large and ungainly double-bed, a four-poster carved out of namwood. It was customary to paint it all over with a bright red lacquer, but if it were made of blackwood (a species of ebony) and boxwood, it was painted with a dark brown lacquer. The front side of the bridal bed was richly carved with discrete panels of floral, figure and animal motifs which, in the case of namwood beds, were richly gilded by thin sheets of gold leaves applied cold over the red lacquer ground. For the wedding ceremonies, the bed was covered all over, from top to bottom, with damask silk or satin drapes profusely embroidered with phoenixes, peonies, quails, mandarin ducks, *ch'i-lings*, dragons and other symbols denoting conjugal fidelity, wedded bliss and prosperity. All this embroidered work was laboriously stitched together by hand using fine needles and coloured silk and gold threads. The Penang State Museum used to display a magnificent example of a richly ornamented peranakan bridal bed completely equipped with all the essential trappings and fineries traditionally used in the marriage ceremonies of those affluent Straits Chinese merchant families. Now the front drapes of the wedding bed are usually drawn aside when the bed is not being used, and they are secured to the two side posts by means of a pair of silvergilt curtain hooks specially made for this purpose.

Such curtain hooks, which always come in pairs, are not, as the name suggests, merely functional devices made strictly for utilitarian ends. On the contrary, judging by the ingenuity and intricacy of the decorative designs, Straits silversmiths must have expended considerable labour and dexterity in fabricating such artefacts, so that among the better pieces, there is the unmistakable stamp of the jeweller's craft. True to peranakan tradition, every item of the richly ornamented bridal bed had to be of the finest craftsmanship that the bride's or groom's family could afford.

Fundamentally, the design of a typical curtain hook intended for the peranakan bridal bed is modelled after the form of a hook-like device. But instead of being content with a plain and functional hook shaped like an inverted question mark, Straits silversmiths fabricated a variety of ornamental panels which were all variations of the basic, ovoidal panels. They then soldered

Fig. 50 This pair of curtain hooks is the work of a highly imaginative silversmith. The upper stem of the hooking device has been skilfully modified to simulate the appearance of a gnarled and twisted branch of the prunus tree with side branches bearing buds and blossoms. The designs are all fashioned in the round, so that both the obverse and reverse sides show identical motifs. Mark of 'Ta Hing'. Silvergilt. Length: 23.5 cm. From Singapore. Author's collection.

these panels on to the vertical stem of the hook. Where the curtain hooks require double-sided ornamental panels, the two identically-carved panels (usually executed in chased and repoussé work) are closely fitted into each other by side flanges and then soldered to the stem of the curtain hook at both ends. The lengths of these panels measure between 10 cm and 16 cm and the decorative motifs usually consist of peonies and phoenixes or simple, conventional floral and foliated patterns executed in chased and relief work. Occasionally one encounters a pair of curtain hooks sporting a combination of pierced and repoussé work on *both* sides of the ornamental panels (see fig. 49). But curtain hooks of this type are uncommon, and they usually show refinement of craftsmanship.

Among the rarer types of curtain hooks, there is one in which the vertical stem of the hook is modified so radically that it transforms into a gnarled and downward-twisting branch of a prunus tree showing buds and flowering blossoms. The lower end of the branch is then extended to form the curving hook. The example shown in fig. 50 was apparently made of beaten silver and fashioned in

the round, so that both the obverse and reverse sides bear identical motifs. But there is no evidence as to where the original seam lines might be, as these would clearly prove that this pair of curtain hooks was originally made in two halves and then soldered together. Nonetheless the solid feel and weight of these hooks give the impression that they had been carved from solid slabs of silver. The four Chinese characters stamped on the top end of the hook read 'Pure Silver' and 'Ta Hing' (大兴), a shop-name which one encounters among the better Straits silver pieces.

The curtain hooks shown in fig. 25 could have been originally made by Chinese silversmiths for wealthy Malay clients. The decorative design of these hooks consists purely of formalized floral and foliated motifs executed on the surface of leaf-shaped panels, and they are shown twining around each other in typical arabesque style. Notice that the design of each of these curtain hooks is so largely taken up by the formalized, leaf-shaped panel of arabesque motifs that the hooks appear to be no more than insignificant appendages attached to the base ends of these panels.

Fig. 51 An ornament for the bridal bed. The Malay and Straits Chinese versions of such ornaments, which were hung from the top of the frontal railing of a four-poster bed, are known as *bekas bunga.* On stylistic evidence alone (e.g., exclusive filigree work, the use of blue enamels and an outer border of *ju-i* motifs) this piece is not of Straits Chinese workmanship. Diameter: 20 cm. Mariette collection.

Ornamental gewgaws

In addition to the standard fittings of the mattress with its embroidered bed sheets, pillows, bolsters and silk drapes, the Straits Chinese bridal bed was also decked with an incredible variety of little fineries and gewgaws. Among the various silver artefacts one finds such curiosities as ornamental bells (some with elaborate tassels), butterfly-shaped panels, and floral caskets known as *bekas bunga* in Malay and *ganchu ranjang* in Baba Malay. Other ornamental hangings include gewgaws of beadwork and silk depicting such auspicious

objects as phoenixes, butterflies, peonies, fishes, starfruits, pomegranates, finger citrons and peaches. All these gaudy baubles were suspended from the canopy, the side posts or the frontal beams of the wedding bed, and, as was customary among the Chinese, these articles always came in pairs.

With regard to those bell-like ornaments, these, too, had no functional significance other than that of giving an added touch of glitter and luxury to the already over-decked interior of the bridal bed. *Bekas bunga* or floral caskets, on the other hand, did serve a useful function. Generally, these artefacts are fashioned after the manner of a stylized flower done in pierced work. The two halves of

Fig. 52 A three-piece set of ornaments for the wedding bed. The large and impressive octagonal piece in the centre is ornamented with repoussé motifs and encloses a small piece embossed with the eight trigrams. The upper attached ornament depicts a pair of bats (omens of good luck) and the lower ornaments depict a fish. Probably a product of South China workmanship. Mariette collection.

these floral caskets are detachable and they are fitted together either by flanges, or by a hinged lid, which can be opened and closed at will. According to an old peranakan custom, it was usual to fill these floral caskets with the heavily scented petals of *bunga chempaka* and *bunga melor*, so that a delicate fragrance would permeate the interior of the bridal bed.

In figs. 53 & 53a we show a pair of fairly large, silvergilt *bekas bunga* crafted in the form of an eight-petalled peony (?) with a prominent, protruding bob in the centre. These floral caskets are made in two detachable halves which are tightly secured together by side flanges. The decorative designs, composed principally of peony and bird

motifs, are finely executed in pierced work on both the obverse and reverse sides. The infinite care with which each spray of peonies is depicted in each of the eight petals is evident. The large octagonal bob is engraved with Taoist emblems (one for each of the eight immortals) on the side panels and bird and flower motifs on the top panel. Suspended from each of the three 'petals' of the caskets are triple tassels with diamond-shaped spangles. The entire casket is in turn suspended from a thicker chain interrupted midway by a pair of castanets.

There is no doubt whatsoever that Straits Chinese floral caskets were inspired by the *bekas bunga* of Malay origin. Ling Roth illustrated a few

Fig. 53 This pair of ornamental caskets, executed in pierced work, is a fine example of *bekas bunga* made to Straits Chinese taste. The caskets are made in two halves and secured together by flanges. In the days gone by, the *bekas bungas* were stuffed with the petals of highly scented flowers, e.g., jasmines. In this way, they served as perfumers inside the wedding bed. Silvergilt. Diameter of caskets: 9 cm. From Singapore. Mrs. Ho Wing Meng.

Fig. 53a Close-up view of the ornamental caskets to show the fine network of floral motifs executed in pierced work.

Fig. 54 An ornamental flower basket executed entirely in filigree work. It is said to have been hung from the canopy of the wedding bed. The uniqueness of this piece of craftsmanship suggests that it is not a product of local silversmiths but rather that of some skilled craftsman in China. It is said to have come from the heirloom of a wealthy Malacca family. A work of great beauty. Silvergilt. Height: 17 cm. Widest width: 10 cm. Weight: 250 gm. Mariette collection.

Fig. 55 Another ornamental flower basket, also executed in filigree work. The elegant eight-sided basket is mounted with a complex of pomegranate flowers (symbols of fertility), while the over-arching handle is surmounted by a pair of phoenixes. Mark of 'Yen Kee'. Height: 18 cm. Weight: 300 gm. Silvergilt. From Malacca. Probably of South China provenance. Mariette collection.

examples of the Malay type of floral caskets in his *Oriental Silverwork*. Now the habit of stuffing such caskets with petals of fragrant flowers was undoubtedly adapted from ancient Malay customs, for there is no evidence of the Chinese in China ever having adopted this practice. Indeed the nearest Chinese counterpart of the *bekas bunga* are miniature flower baskets, some of which are crafted entirely in filigree work. But flower baskets of this sort were not meant to be mere receptacles for holding stuffed petals of fragrant flowers – they were actual representation in miniature of flower baskets made of solid pieces of silver. The two delightful flower baskets shown in figs. 54 & 55 convey some idea of the splendour and jewel-like quality of fine Chinese silverwork.

The practice of stuffing fragrant flowers into ornamental silver receptacles hung inside the wedding bed was probably peculiar to Malay customs; for there is no evidence that the Chinese in China ever observed this practice. For this reason, too, any silver box or container made of pierced work and suspended from chains was usually described as an 'incense burner'. In the Carl Kempe collection of ancient Chinese silverwork, there is a globular incense burner with pierced work designs, fashioned in two detachable halves and suspended from a chain. While it is possible to burn incense inside these burners, it is undesirable to do so under warm, tropical conditions. Besides, the presence of live embers inside a burner definitely increases the risk of a fire, especially when the bridal bed was covered with silk and satin fabrics.

Fig. 56 A pair of ornamental bell-like objects probably used to adorn the wedding bed. The decorative motifs are done in chased work. The long tassels and spangles are typical of such ornaments. Silvergilt. Length including tassels: 20 cm. Diameter of 'bells': 6 cm. From Singapore. Mrs. Ho Wing Meng.

Fig. 57 Another pair of bell-like ornaments, in hexagonal shapes. Though they look like bells, they were not made to tinkle. Silvergilt. Length including tassels: 12 cm. From Singapore. Mrs. Ho Wing Meng.

Floral caskets of the *bekas bunga* type are so few and far between (I have not encountered more than three pairs in all these years) that several people to whom I originally showed these articles were unable to say what functional purposes they served. It is probable that *bekas bungas* were not commonly employed even by the wealthy peranakan Chinese. The same might be said of those bell-shaped ornaments (see figs. 56 & 57). There are no related counterparts of these objects among ancient Chinese silverwork nor those of Malay origin; and since they were not intended to chime or tinkle, the conclusion must be that they merely served as splendid baubles.

Among old family heirlooms in several parts of Johore and Malacca, one occasionally encounters another type of hanging ornaments consisting of three rosette, leaf-shaped or a combination of rosette and leaf-shaped medallions, all connected by intricate tassels. These hanging ornaments always come in pairs, and they are mostly gilded and decorated exclusively with floral and foliated designs on both the obverse and reverse sides. The technique of execution was a combination of pierced and repoussé work. By and large the workmanship is of an indifferent quality, and the majority of antique dealers and silversmiths whom we consulted maintained that they were made by Chinese craftsmen of a bygone era. Such ornaments, too, were intended to adorn the bridal bed. The three medallions were intended to signify the Three Abundances, namely, Good Luck, Prosperity and Longevity.

Filigree work

For some reason or other which has never been entirely clear to me, Straits Chinese silversmiths throughout the nineteenth century appeared to have avoided as much as possible the technique of filigree work in all their artefacts. It is true, as Dr. Bo Gyllensvard noted in an earlier work, that from about the eighteenth century onwards, the repoussé technique of ornamenting silverwork came to be widely adopted by Chinese goldsmiths and silversmiths. Since the traditional Chinese have an ingrained habit of perpetuating for as long as possible some successful artistic tradition, it is to be expected that the popularity of the repoussé technique would have been carried on into the nineteenth century, as extant examples of nineteenth-century Chinese trade silverwork exported to Europe and America clearly testify. The same may be said of nineteenth-century Straits Chinese silver in Malaya, especially the former Straits Settlement colonies of Singapore, Malacca and Penang.

Now the filigree technique, which consists largely of soldering various lengths of silver wires to create aesthetic designs, was a very ancient one known to goldsmiths and silversmiths from time immemorial. And from an aesthetic point of view, filigree designs are no less satisfying than chased work, repoussé work, engraving or appliqué work, as the two flower baskets in figs. 54 & 55 clearly show. Furthermore, the emergence of the repoussé technique as the most popular method of embellishing silverwork did not, as was to be expected in a vast country like China where tradition dies hard, cause the total demise of the ancient technique of filigree work. The proof of it is that some, if not all of those migrant Chinese silversmiths who came to the Straits Settlements during the course of the nineteenth century did, in fact, demonstrate evidence of their ability to work successfully in the filigree technique, as the pieces in figs. 58 & 59 indicate. There is no doubt, therefore, that this familiarity with the method of filigree work may be attributed to the fact that all Straits Chinese silversmiths, irrespective of whether they had originally been trained in China or else acquired the skill through apprenticeship with some local master craftsmen, underwent the same kind of training which their forebears had acquired before them.

Fig. 58 This multi-chained wedding necklace for the Straits Chinese bride is embellished by a variety of ten different kinds of decorative panels, executed entirely in filigree work, and interspersed at regular intervals. The sheer splendour of the design reminds one of those elaborate necklaces made for ancient Egyptian and Middle Eastern queens and nobility. Silvergilt. From Malacca. Mariette collection.

Fig. 59 This unusual neck or collar ornament is made up of a circular collar with an extended tongue-like appendage. The various decorative panels sporting filigree motifs are sewn on to a backing of red velvet and cotton fabrics. Length: 28 cm. From Malacca.

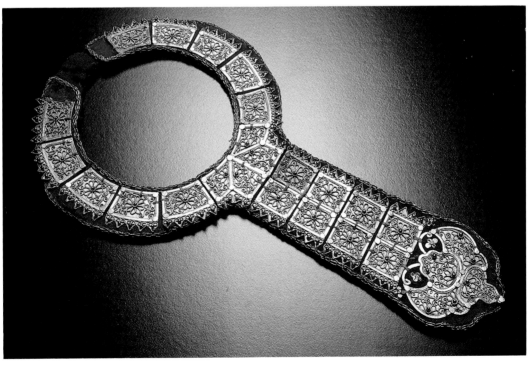

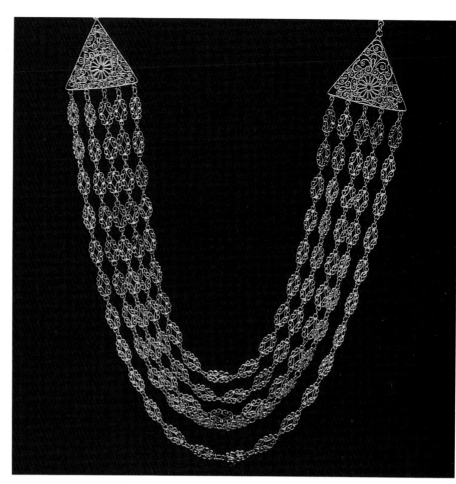

Fig. 60   A Straits Chinese bridal necklace consisting of five parallel chains suspended from two rectangular plaques executed in pierced work. Silvergilt. From Malacca. Mariette collection.

Fig. 61   Another example of multi-chained necklace of simple elegance. The various chains are made up of little florets executed in pierced work and connected together by tiny rings. Silvergilt. From Malacca. Mariette collection.

Nonetheless the fact remains that among extant pieces of Straits silverwork, the application of the filigree technique was relatively infrequent and usually confined to items of jewellery and articles of *virtu*. Why is that so? Apart from the fact that the repoussé technique of ornamentation was in vogue throughout the eighteenth and the nineteenth century, there was this well-known habit among the more affluent class of Straits Chinese nonyas, to flaunt their wealth by wearing ornate and impressive items of jewellery and other personal ornaments. As every student of gold and silver knows too well, no other technique of ornamentation is calculated to project the scintillating qualities of gold and silver more dramatically than the art of repoussé work. It is no coincidence,

Fig. 62 A beaded necklace made up of graduated silver beads executed in a combination of pierced and appliqué work. Necklaces of this design probably had their origin in the Middle East or Eastern Europe. It was popular in Bohemia. Silvergilt. From Malacca. Mariette collection.

therefore, that the Straits nonyas took to gold and silver articles ornamented in repoussé work like ducks to water.

Filigree work, by comparison, is somewhat more subdued and understated. You have to look hard and carefully to appreciate the subtle nuances of the craftsman's skill. Besides, working in the filigree technique is at best a tedious and time-consuming process. In particular, the delicate task of cutting, joining, twisting, twirling and soldering innumerable lengths of silver wires can tax even the patience of a saint. In any case, the Straits nonyas, who constituted the wealthiest patrons of the goldsmith and silversmith, did not fancy the quiet beauty of filigree work.

In figs. 60–62 we illustrate some examples of filigree work which were fabricated locally by Chinese silversmiths in Johore or Malacca. Notice that most of these articles which sport filigree ornamental work are small and generally confined to items of jewellery such as hairpins, necklaces, pendants and brooches. By and large filigree work is often used in combination with chased, repoussé, engraving and also appliqué work. The two flower baskets shown in figs. 54 & 55 are very good examples of the predominant application of the filigree technique in combination with repoussé work. But they were probably made in Shanghai or Peking for export to Southeast Asia.

ITEMS OF PERSONAL ORNAMENTS

By far the commonest items of silverwork turned out by local Chinese silversmiths during the nineteenth century were articles of personal ornaments intended for nonyas, who were particularly fond of gold and silver jewellery of ingenious and intricate workmanship. Although these items of jewellery were intended both for daily use as well as for formal, ceremonial occasions, those of better quality (especially those made of gold) were used for festive celebrations such as the Chinese New Year, birthdays, anniversaries, weddings and even funerals.

To list but some of the ceremonial accoutrements of the Straits Chinese bride: her head-dress, if she happened to come from a well-to-do family, consisted of a high-domed diadem made of some felt or velvet fabric superimposed with a semi-globular network of silver ornaments, comprising chiefly of phoenixes and peacocks, peonies, butterflies, pomegranates, and Buddhist and Taoist emblems of blessing, good luck and prosperity. Very few of these wedding coronets for the bride have survived intact: the relics of some of these impressive head-dresses that I have seen in the past were in bits and pieces, and were it not for the fact that wedding pictures of peranakan grooms and brides dating back to the 'nineties of the last century are still available, one would have to rely entirely upon one's imagination to reconstruct shapes of these wedding head-dresses. Likewise hardly any of the headgear worn by the groom chiefly in the form of the Manchu summer cap with broad, up-turned brim, have survived to this day. The few caps with beads and embroidered patterns were probably intended for the page-boy.

Around the bride's neck, in addition to an intricate collar-piece of beads and embroidered work, a gold or silver chain with a matching pendant of ornate workmanship, she wore a broad multi-chained necklace made of elaborate rosettes mounted with precious stones and linked together by hundreds of tiny, hand-crafted rings. She might also wear between four and eight more silvergilt or gold chains to impress upon her husband's family and relatives that she was amply provided for by her family! As a predominantly merchant and trading community without any pretensions to hereditary nobility or scholarly accomplishments, the peranakan Chinese were very conscious of material wealth which they flaunted so ostentatiously at wedding ceremonies.

Other essential accoutrements of the bridal costume included a pair of drop earrings usually set with pearls, diamonds, emeralds or rubies. On her wrists the bride wore a varied assortment of bangles and bracelets, all of which must come in pairs or multiples of two. Two pairs of identical wedding rings were worn on the third and fourth fingers of each hand respectively. Around her waist (if she happened to change to *sarong* and *baju kurong* or *sarong* and *kebaya*) the bride, as well as the groom, each wore a broad and elaborately crafted silver (or even gold) belt held together by an equally ornate, ogival-shaped buckle of impressive workmanship. And following the ancient Hindu-Islamic custom, the wearing of anklets was obligatory. Let us now examine in greater detail some of the salient features in the design and craftsmanship of these articles in the traditional bridal trousseau of the peranakan Chinese.

Fig. 63 Here are three different types of Straits Chinese belts with matching buckles. The belt on the extreme right is solidly constructed out of specially-designed interlocking links arranged in such a way as to simulate the texture of woven grass mats. The topmost belt, on the other hand, gives the appearance of pleated silver wires, while the left belt consists of separate segments fabricated out of stiffened silver wires and reinforced by appliqued butterfly motifs. Mariette collection.

Belts and buckles

Belts

Belts and buckles are among the most conspicuous articles of personal ornaments made for the peranakan Chinese. The typical silver belt, for example, is noted for its ingenuity of design and intricacy of workmanship. Basically, this consists of a flexible band composed of a network of up to several thousand pieces of interlocking rings or links of various shapes arranged to form a regular pattern of some sort, and superimposed at regular intervals on the obverse side, with granulé work, pieces of rosettes and other geometrical ornaments, all of which are individually crafted and soldered on to the surface of the belt (see figs. 63 & 64). Occasionally one encounters belts which are

fabricated out of four or more thick strands of silver, each of which is twisted out of fine silver wires. The various strands are laid side by side and then tightly clamped together by decorative clasps distributed at regular intervals throughout the entire length of the belt. Such belts, including those which were fabricated to simulate the textures of woven grass mats or woven fabrics (see fig. 65), were not worn by the nonyas; in fact, they were made by Chinese silversmiths in Sarawak for the Ibans, the Dayaks and other native tribes who were equally noted for their fondness of silver ornaments. Mostly, these belts were made to order. While there is no standard length for a belt, the widths varied between 3 cm and 5 cm on the average. Both ends of the belts are neatly finished with the necessary catches or hooks for attaching the buckle.

Fig. 64 A set of typical Straits Chinese belt and buckle of good craftsmanship. The belt is entirely fabricated out of a network of interlocking rings superimposed on the obverse surface with little diamond panels and florets done in appliqué work. Silvergilt. From Singapore. Mrs. Ho Wing Meng.

Fig. 65 The two impressive sets of belts and buckles shown in this picture are not of Straits Chinese origin. They were made by Chinese silversmiths in Sarawak (East Malaysia) for wealthy Chinese, Dayak and Iban chiefs, and the overall design of these works are more Chinese than Malay in taste. Notice that the belts tend to be fitted with additional decorative panels, apparently to evoke an air of barbarian splendour about them. The buckles tend to be squarish. From Sarawak. Mariette collection.

The making of one of these belts involved a considerable amount of time-consuming labour, as all the various parts had to be individually handcrafted. An average belt, for example, required on the average over one thousand pieces of interlocking rings and links of various shapes, and these pieces had to be arranged to form a decorative pattern. With belts of larger dimensions (intended for more ample nonyas!) more than two thousand pieces had to be individually crafted and painstakingly assembled to make one of these articles. Of course, in the days when nothing moved faster than a horse carriage, and mechanization of labour was practically unheard of in Malaya, skilled silversmiths did not baulk at the prospect of spending weeks and months labouring over a single article. Nonetheless the work was tedious and often taxing in terms of skill and patience, while the rewards for their labours were probably minimal.

For this reason, as the demands for silver belts of such intricate workmanship increased during the course of the nineteenth century, Straits silversmiths had to think of ways and means of increas-

Fig. 66 The belt illustrated here is unexceptional where Straits Chinese belts are concerned. From a technical point of view, however, this belt represents a later stage in the art of fabricating what I would like to call 'prefabricated belts'. In applying this technique of prefabrication, the silversmith dispenses entirely with the traditional method of constructing a belt by painstakingly soldering together a bewildering number of tiny pieces of interlocking rings and appliqued rosettes. Instead, he constructs the belt by linking together a series of relatively large rectangular panels (about 3.5 cm by 3 cm) which have previously been ornamented with formalized floral motifs executed in a combination of repoussé and pierced work. From Singapore. Mrs. Ho Wing Meng.

ing their productive capacity without being bogged down by the more tedious and unproductive methods of traditional craftsmanship. One method was to dispense with the need of fabricating and individually assembling thousands of interlocking bits and pieces including those appliqued pieces of rosettes, and instead to construct the belt out of relatively large rectangular, oval or octagonal panels and then joining them together by a smaller number of links (see fig. 66). Such panels may be decorated with pierced, appliqué, chased or repoussé designs of various degrees of complexity and refinement. In this way the silversmith obviated the tedium of working on minutiae, for the new-styled belts required at the most only between 30 and 40 pieces of such panels arranged in serial order to make a belt of average size. On the other hand, the saving effected in time and labour enabled the craftsman to increase efficiency and output. It is not known, however, whether division of labour was practised in any extensive way for the fabrication of these belts of more recent designs. But it would be surprising, indeed, if labour-saving methods were not employed, given the strong, profit-making motive and ingenious skill of the traditional Chinese silversmith.

Buckles

It is in the fabrication of those large, ogival-shaped buckles with a pronounced, convex surface and very intricately carved designs that Straits Chinese silversmiths displayed the mastery of their craftsmanship in a most consummate fashion. Here the skill and patience required were even more exacting, for these buckles required the representation of a variety of decorative motifs arranged in some complex, but auspiciously appropriate, pattern. But as with other categories of Straits silver, not every extant piece of peranakan-styled buckle showed the same consistency of finish and refinement. Some of the later pieces showed all the defects of hasty and shoddy workmanship.

Straits Chinese buckles come in several different forms; the most common being of quatre-

Fig. 67 Of the three buckles shown here, the top two are not in Straits Chinese taste. They were probably the products of Chinese silversmiths in Sarawak, East Malaysia; and in the days gone by, such buckles were particularly popular with the Ibans and other well-to-do tribal chiefs from the interiors of Sarawak. The buckle below is, of course, in typical nonya taste, and it is exhibited here to distinguish Straits Chinese buckles from those of other provenance. Mariette et al.

Fig. 68 This lovely, ogival-shaped buckle of Straits Chinese workmanship sports a pronounced convex surface after the manner of old Malay-Sumatran buckles (see figs. 27 & 28). However the surface is modified to incorporate an incredible variety of auspicious Chinese symbols, particularly the ubiquitous pair of phoenixes and peony blossoms. The fine and realistic motifs are carved in high reliefs: notice that unmistakable deftness and sureness of touch in the craftsmanship. This was intended to be a wedding buckle for the groom and was originally gilded. Length: 16 cm. Width: 11.5 cm. From Malacca. Mrs. Ho Wing Meng.

foil shape. However a typical Straits Chinese buckle closely resembling one of Malay origin is ovoidal or ogival in shape. From time to time one encounters some large buckles which are modelled after the form of a half-opened scroll ornamented with figure and floral motifs executed in chased and repoussé work. These buckles are not of Straits Chinese taste and they were not, as a rule, made in the Straits Settlements. Most of them came from Sarawak and Sabah, and were in fact made by local Chinese silversmiths. The principal clients of Chinese silverwork in Sarawak and Sabah were Chinese *towkays* (merchants), Dayak

and Iban native chiefs (see figs. 65 & 67). Silverwork fabricated in Sarawak and Sabah appeared to have been more conservatively Chinese in taste – there being no evidence of old Malay influence either in the shapes of these articles or in the contents of the ornamental motifs.

The buckle shown in fig. 31 is probably one of the finest examples of the remarkable talents of Straits silversmiths, though two other buckles, one in silver (fig. 68) and one in gold (fig. 30) come close to rival it in the beauty and exuberance and precision of workmanship. Notice that although a casual glance at this buckle may give the impression of dazzling complexity, there is, in fact, nothing haphazard or capricious about the manner in which the various sets of decorative motifs are selected and represented here. On the contrary, a closer inspection soon reveals that the types of decorative motifs chosen for representation in this buckle were made according to certain unstated rules of propitiousness and then systematically arranged. Once we recognize the symbolic significance of the various motifs thus chosen, we can see that the plan of the decorative design is quite simply articulated.

Firstly, there is a small circular panel at the centre enclosing a writhing dragon chasing after the legendary pearl. Secondly, surrounding this central panel is a much larger rosette band incorporating the figures of the eight Taoist immortals, depicted in pairs and arranged on the four cardinal points of the compass. The intervening spaces between these figures are filled with flowers of the four seasons. Thirdly, the rosette band is bounded by the third and outermost band of ogival shape. This outermost band contains a profusion of some very interesting and auspiciously significant motifs executed with realism and precision workmanship. The objects include dragons, phoenixes, fishes, stags, peonies, pine trees and prunus trees. The repoussé work of this buckle is depicted in such high reliefs and life-like vigour, that when viewed under a low-powered magnifying glass, one gets the impression that the fishes, the dragons and the phoenixes are about to leap out of the matrix in which they take their forms. The craftsman who fabricated this buckle must have derived considerable satisfaction from the expo-

sition of this masterly feat of craftsmanship in miniature.

It is true that in this particular article, as well as in the majority of the finer pieces of Straits silverwork, the tendency to opt for variety and complexity of ornamental motifs invariably gives these artefacts an overwhelming impression of overwrought complexity – an effect often decried by those who prefer simplicity and unity of design. Straits Chinese silverwork, however, merely reflected the prevailing tastes of the Ch'ing period which, during the reign of Ch'ien Lung (1736–95) particularly, regarded refinement and ornateness of workmanship as the criteria of artistic excellence. It so happened that the preference for chased and repoussé work of great intricacy as manifested in Straits silverwork found immediate appeal with the peranakan womenfolk whose fondness for conspicuous display was nowhere more vividly gratified than in these large ogival buckles which sometimes measure up to 17 cm in length and 12 cm in width.

The very wealthy babas naturally had their ceremonial buckles fashioned out of gold, though extant pieces of gold buckles appear to be very rare – I do not recall having seen more than six pieces of gold buckles in Straits Chinese style during the course of the past ten years. But judging by the oral testimonies of the older generations of surviving peranakans, as well as by the descriptions of Straits Chinese weddings given by various writers, the use of such gold buckles must have been fairly common with wealthy Straits Chinese families. That so very few of these artefacts have survived to this day indicates that many

Fig. 69 Here are some of the commoner and smaller versions of Straits Chinese buckles that are frequently encountered in silversmiths in Singapore, Johore and Malacca until about fifteen years ago. The motifs consist mostly of phoenixes, *ch'i-lings* and peony blossoms. Length of the largest buckle: 8 cm. From Singapore. Mrs. Ho Wing Meng and Mariette.

Fig. 70 Here are two characteristic nonya purses, each of which is suspended by chains attached at the topmost end to a clip which can be inserted into the side of a silver belt. The pouch of a typical nonya purse is made up of a flexible network of rosettes, stars and florets, all interconnected by little rings and suspended from a stiff, inverted 'u'-shaped spine. Such purses were inspired by Victorian ladies' purses, but differ from them by being generally smaller in size, and sporting decorative motifs which are purely Chinese in origin. Length including chain: 20 cm. Width averages around 9 cm. From Singapore. Mariette collection.

of these priceless articles must have been sold in times of pressing circumstances to goldsmiths and pawnshops to recover their bullion value. The subsequent fate of these articles can well be imagined: the goldsmiths would normally retain these articles as long as there was a demand for them. The moment he sensed that these artefacts had become passé he consigned them to the melting crucible, and in this manner some of the most irreplaceable works of art were lost beyond recall.

For the Straits nonyas of average means in those days, the type of buckle that was coupled to their silvergilt belts was a smaller, ogival or quatrefoil-shaped article of simpler workmanship (see fig. 69). The average length of such buckles is 9.5 cm and about 8 cm in width. The quality of the workmanship varied from one silversmith to another, the examples shown in fig. 69 being of better quality than those run-of-the-mill type of buckles of this shape.

Ladies' purses

The traditional nonyas did not carry handbags of any sort. Those silver handbags or purses suspended from a chain were copied from similar silver handbags or purses made for English ladies during the Victorian era. Only the more anglicized of Straits nonyas used such silver handbags on formal occasions. For this reason, locally-made Victorian-styled, silver handbags are not frequently seen among Straits silverwork.

The typical nonya purse in those days consisted of a small rectangular pouch made of silver wirework consisting of a net of very small interlocking rings and appliqued rosette ornaments suspended from two neatly-fitted and stiffly-constructed frames pivoted at both extremities, so that they can be opened and shut at will. The sizes of the pouches vary, but the average pouch measures 10 cm long and 9 cm wide. Two hanging chains attached to the top of the supporting frames are connected to an ornamental clip which can be inserted into the side of the belt. The nonya purse

was always suspended from either the right or the left side of the silver belt; it was never carried by hand, at least not until Straits silversmiths made copies of Victorian handbags.

The resemblance between the nonya silver purse and the Victorian period silver handbag was not a fortuitous one; from a purely stylistic point of view, the nonya silver purse was derived from its English version some time during the nineteenth century, except that the Straits silversmith modified the general design of the Victorian handbag to suit the needs of the peranakan womenfolk. A close inspection of a typical nonya purse as shown in fig. 70 will reveal this fact at once. Notice that the pouch is made up of a network of hundreds of little, circular interlocking rings superimposed on the external surface with a variety of starlets, rosettes or diamond-shaped spangles arranged in regular rows. The bottom of the pouch is usually embellished with a row of almond-shaped spangles. The two short chains suspending the purse are held together by an ornamental clip which is chased with typical Chinese floral and foliated motifs.

Needless to say, the fabrication of one of these little silver purses involved a great deal of skilled craftsmanship and patience: for one thing, those little circular rings had to be fabricated individually and then assembled into a complex network by hand. Those little star- and almond-shaped spangles had also to be cut from thin pieces of silver plate and then manually soldered on to the surface of the pouch. No wonder these delicately-crafted silver purses quickly went out of fashion as soon as large leather handbags and

Fig. 71 From an artistic point of view, there is perhaps nothing remarkable about this Victorian-inspired nonya purse. However, when you begin to scrutinize the pouch carefully, you soon realize that it is made up of a fine network of tiny, hand-made silver rings – in fact, well over 5,500 individually soldered miniature rings ingeniously interlocked to give flexibility to the pouch! How much time, you may ask, was expended in putting together a network of 5,500 tiny, interlocking silver rings? Length: 15 cm. Width: 12.5 cm. From Singapore. Mrs. Ho Wing Meng.

beadwork handbags came on the scene. Nonya silver purses had one other drawback: they were far too small and delicate to withstand the wear and tear of daily use.

The handbag shown in fig. 71 is probably a late nineteenth-century imitation of Victorian period handbags. It measures 15 cm by 12.5 cm, and it is large as far as nonya purses go. But the remarkable thing about this handbag is the elaborate network of the pouch which is made up of about 5,500 pieces of tiny hand-crafted, interlocking rings, each of which is no more than 3 mm in diameter. How much time was expended in the making of these hanging pouches is anybody's guess, but there is no doubt that they were the works of what is now a bygone breed of vanished silversmiths. One wonders in these days of labour shortage and premium wages for skilled labour, what it would cost just to commission a silversmith to make a nonya purse of this sort by painstaking manual labour.

Fig. 72 A bridal purse and a set of ornamented silver panels without the usual fabric backings. The pierced-work motifs on all the four decorated panels are crafted to a high degree of craftsmanship – indications that these purses were commissioned for wealthy baba clients. The flap-panel on the right is unique in depicting the traditional *San Twoh* or Three Abundances theme. Silvergilt. Mark of 'Ta Hing' stamped on the right panels. Length: 12 cm. From Malacca. Mariette et al.

The so-called 'pocket plaques'

In the previous edition of this book, under the heading 'Miscellaneous Items', I referred to a particular category of Straits silver plates which, to all intents and purposes, look like pocket plaques, and were in fact described as such. I have since then discovered that my original description was erroneous. Actually, these so-called 'pocket plaques' had never been stitched on to the pockets of ceremonial costumes of any sort. It was Mrs. Mariette who drew my attention to this error recently when she showed me several purses from her collection, one of which had silver plaques very similar to those shown in figs. 149 and

150 of the previous edition, stitched on to lovely red velvet backings ornamented on the reverse side with floral designs executed in tiny metal beads. This exceptional purse (see fig. 72) was fabricated in such a way that the silver plaque similar to the one in fig. 149, was sewn on to the velvet-and-felt backing to form the flap or cover of the purse. The other plaque, also resembling the one in fig. 150, was sewn on to a similarly-shaped velvet backing to form the pouch. Purses of this type were made to be inserted either into a silvergilt belt, or a belt executed with beadwork on velvet and canvas backing. Figs. 72 & 73 of the present edition show two examples of these splendid purses. In Mrs. Queeny Chang's recent book[25] there is also a similar velvet purse of this sort embroidered with a mixture of tiny, but brightly-

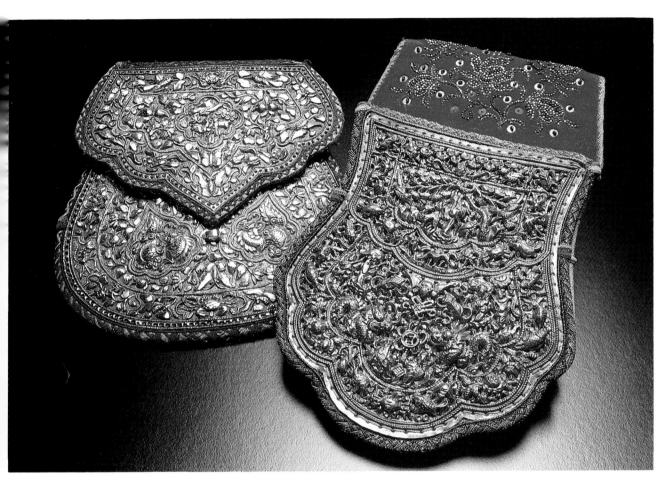

Fig. 73 Two wedding purses, one for the bride (left) and the other for the groom (right), fabricated out of pre-ornamented silver panels which are then sewn on to backings of felt, silk and cotton fabrics. The silver panels of the bride's purse are executed in repoussé motifs, while the panel on the groom's purse is executed in pierced work. The back of the groom's purse is further embroidered with small metal beads. Such purses are inserted into the wedding belt. Length of larger purse: 12 cm. From Malacca. Mariette collection.

coloured, glass beads. Since this purse was among exhibits of her personal mementos, we may presume that it was used by her on her wedding.

Purses of this type which come intact with their silver plaques attached to their velvet-and-felt backings and beaded decorations, are rarely encountered nowadays, even though they must have been as common as hairpins, brooches, belts and buckles. After all, many of the well-to-do, but traditional, Straits Chinese families in the Straits Settlements adhered to their ancient wedding customs up till the 'twenties of the present century. But because velvets and felts deteriorate very rapidly under the warm and humid climate in the tropics, including attacks by silverfish and other insects, very few of these purses have survived in their pristine conditions.

The bigger of these purses, especially those with flaps, were presumably worn by the groom, while the smaller ones without flaps were used by the bride; provided, that is, both bride and groom wore the traditional, two-piece ceremonial costumes consisting of a long-sleeved garment and an ankle-length skirt. The differences between the groom's costume and that of the bride lie in the more elaborately ornamented, embroidered designs of the bride's costume, the great length of the garment and the additional layers and/or pleats in the bridal skirt. Since the skirts worn both by the bride and the groom had to be secured around the waist by a belt of some sort, it was considered appropriate to include one of these splendid purses as part of the ceremonial accoutrements.

Most of the plaques made for such ceremonial purses are very ornately ornamented with the usual types of decorative motifs including phoenixes, dragons, peonies, plum blossoms, bats and butterflies, executed in pierced and repoussé work. I have not encountered purse plaques done exclusively in chased or repoussé work. This may be attributed to the fact that silvergilt plaques decorated with pierced work probably look better when set against a background of crimson or scarlet velvet and felt. The two plaques shown in fig. 72 (right) clearly belong together, as they form the panels for the flap and the pouch of a purse. The workmanship here is much more refined than that of the more common run of purse plaques.

If we examine the motifs on the two plaques in some detail, it soon becomes apparent that the flap plaque depicts the theme of the *San Twoh* (三多) or, in other words, the three most desirable things in life, namely, material wealth, many sons and long life. This is simply represented here by a set of three figures (reading from right to left) consisting, firstly, of a person dressed in an official mandarin robe (notice the cap with the two fan-like projections) accompanied by an umbrella-bearing attendant; secondly, an old bearded man sitting on a throne and flanked on either side by symbols of longevity, namely, a stork and a stag; and thirdly, a woman holding a child and attended by a servant. The first represents wealth and success, the second, longevity and the third, many sons.

The motif on the pouch-plaque is ornamented somewhat differently: it depicts two writhing dragons pursuing the legendary flaming pearl amidst swirls of waves and fire. Two coins, signifying riches, and a hovering bat, signifying good luck, fill up the rest of the space. The two broad borders are filled with trailing floral and foliated motifs. Notice the lace-like quality about the pierced and repoussé motifs. The gilding has a reddish hue.

Keyholders

Basically, the peranakan-styled keyholder is made up of a broad oval clip with a ring attached to the base-end of the clip. Unlike the standard, functional metal ring which can be operated in a variety of ways to hold a bunch of keys, the Straits Chinese keyholder had to be re-designed and modified to incorporate a ring attached to a broad, ornately carved ornamental clip in order to satisfy the peranakan's obsession with artifice rather than with functional requirements. Accordingly, Straits silversmiths modelled the frontal side of the broad clip to include a decorative panel, usually of ogival shape, and worked into it various auspicious symbols such as peonies, fishes, phoenixes, butterflies and even figure motifs executed in a combination of pierced and repoussé work. The main ornamental panel is worked in such a way that it presents a pronounced, convex surface separately crafted and then soldered on to the flat surface of the broad clip. In this way, Straits Chinese keyholders have a solid, three-dimensional feel about them.

The top end of this decorative panel is usually surmounted by a single motif consisting of either a crab, a bat or, in some instances, the grinning

Fig. 74 Here is an assortment of eight typical Straits Chinese keyholders. The largest among them (top) is a refined piece of craftsmanship executed in a combination of pierced and repoussé work. I have often wondered about the origins of such Straits Chinese keyholders, because I have not seen keyholders of Chinese or Malay origin which might have served as archetypes of these articles. Length of the largest keyholder is 9 cm, while that of the smallest is 6 cm. From Singapore.

human mask of some sort. This object is always carved in the round. Panels decorated with exclusively repoussé motifs are rare; most of the Straits nonyas in those days preferred to have keyholders with designs of pierced work because pierced work lent a delicate, tracery texture to the workmanship. Fig. 74 shows a collection of typical Straits Chinese keyholders frequently encountered in old silversmiths.

Notice that apart from the standard peranakan type of keyholders featuring predominantly floral and foliated motifs, there are some sporting a variety of ornamented panels including the shape of a carp, a vase, a double gourd and, in rare instances, the figure of a man or deity riding on the back of a carp. Such unusual keyholders probably appealed to the non-peranakan clients who could perhaps appreciate the symbolic significance of these esoteric motifs better than the more Malayanized nonyas themselves. But the

craftsmanship of such keyholders are alike attributable to local silversmiths. Keyholders also vary very greatly in their sizes. There were no standard sizes for such utensils. The largest encountered measures 9 cm long, while the smallest of them is about 6 cm. Although the difference in length between the largest and the smallest of keyholders is only slightly over 2.5 cm, the overall difference is quite noticeable.

If one studies carefully the topmost keyholder in fig. 74 one will notice that it belongs to one of the larger varieties of Straits Chinese keyholders which sport a modified, ogival panel with a pronounced convex surface carved with two fishes (one of which looks like the sturgeon of the Huang-ho River) swimming among water weeds. This central motif is enclosed by a delicate border of plum blossoms, and the techniques employed here are pierced and relief work. The workmanship is superb, especially with regard to the precise representations of the various motifs and the refinement of the finish. The unusual feature about this keyholder is the ornamental motif surmounting the top of the decorative panel: it depicts a grotesque, human mask with exaggerated features typical of those fearsome *t'ao-tieh* masks of ancient Shang bronze vessels, except that this one appears to be the grinning visage of some spiritual being.

There is, as far as I know, no evidence to show that keyholders were exclusively intended for Straits nonyas. This is because the carrying of keys was not confined to nonyas alone. The men used them also. However, from about the second half of the nineteenth century, most of the English-educated babas switched to wearing English-styled costumes. This meant that they could no longer wear those silver belts made of more 'masculine' designs, and the result was that keyholders with those typical ornamental clips fell out of fashion – at least as far as the babas were concerned. Of course, the more conservative of the baba merchants and traders who adhered to the habit of wearing the typically loose tunic with long sleeves and baggy trousers could continue to wear either silver belts or those broad leather belts. For these people the large keyholders continued to serve a useful function, since they could be clipped on to the belt.

JEWELLERY

Most extant items of Straits Chinese jewellery (and I include under this heading such things as brooches, necklaces, hairpins, pendants, earrings, finger-rings, bracelets and anklets) share common characteristics of resemblance with similar articles made formerly for Malay, Sumatran and Javanese women of aristocratic birth. This is entirely consistent with the view I hold, namely, that Straits Chinese culture was largely influenced by ancient Hindu-Islamic customs and traditions. Since the earliest of Straits nonyas were probably of native origin, it was only natural that the designs of their jewellery should be greatly inspired by old Malay, Sumatran or Javanese archetypes. In matters of decorative details, however, traditional Chinese art and religious symbols were commonly adopted, except brooches and hairpins where purely floral and foliated motifs were preferred. Here it may be noted that Straits silversmiths applied the well-known jeweller's techniques of chasing, embossing, engraving and filigree work in addition to the standard methods of granulation work, box-setting, *à jour* setting for mounting and beautifying precious and semi-precious stones.

For some unknown reasons, however, I have never been able to find enamelling and *niello* works employed in those items of jewellery intended for the Straits nonyas, although these techniques were well-known to Chinese silversmiths and other metal workers for decorating cloisonné ornaments and utensils. As for the technique of enamelling silverwork (or gold), from the time of the Ming Dynasty, Chinese craftsmen introduced the brilliant blue kingfisher feathers for coating items of jewellery intended for royalty. In the Ting Ling Underground Palace mausoleum of the Emperor Wan-li (1573–1619) in Peking, for example, are two magnificent crowns of Wan-li's two empresses studded with phoenixes and peacocks enamelled in brilliant kingfisher feathers. Subsequently, this innovation was widely adopted for the ornamental headgear of royalty and nobility of the Ch'ing Dynasty.

Nearer home, in Sumatra, Thailand and Java, *niello* work was popular with the natives of these countries. In particular, the products of Palembang silversmiths (e.g., those great ogival buckles, finger bowls and slender pear-shaped bottles) were exceedingly beautiful. It may be that the Straits nonyas, noted for their fondness of diamonds, rubies, emeralds and sapphires, must have regarded enamelling as a cheap and unsatisfactory method of beautifying jewellery. Besides the bluish-black background of Sumatran and Malayan *niello* work tended to give a dark and subdued appearance rather than a brilliant and dazzling surface. In any case, it was taboo to wear black on the wedding day.

The wealthier babas were particularly snobbish about their tastes for diamonds, rubies and emeralds. But by and large, the various articles of jewellery in existence and which traditionally formed the standard ornaments of the Straits nonyas were decorated with a type of low quality, industrial diamonds, irregularly shaped and faceted, known as 'intans'. These were imported from various parts of Kalimantan including the areas around Pontianak and Banjermasin. They look more like rough-cut industrial diamonds or zircons. Pearls of the baroque variety with a yellowish lustre were also popular with the nonyas.

But jade, whether the green variety of jadeite from Burma or the multi-coloured nephrite from Turkestan, was largely ignored, probably because jade does not have the 'fire' of sparkling gems.

Brooches

The traditional nonya brooches or *kerosangs* always came in sets of three; these consist of either three identical, ring-shaped brooches or, alternatively, a relatively large heart-shaped brooch matched with two circular ones. The more eccentric ones are shaped like finger citrons, insects or an oval network of floral and foliated motifs executed in cutwork. Until about the opening decade of the present century, these antique *kerosangs* were traditionally used for several hundred years by the nonyas, both young and old alike, to secure as well as to adorn the frontal hems of the *baju kurong*, the standard costume of all Malay and Straits Chinese women.

However, with the introduction of the more elegant *sarong kebaya* at about the time of the First World War (from Medan?), most of the younger generation of nonyas discarded their traditional *baju kurong* in favour of the newer form of personal attire. They also cast aside those 'old-fashioned' circular and heart-shaped *kerosangs*.[26] Most of the older and more conservative generations of nonyas, however, would not modernize their dress style; so they stuck to their *baju kurong* costumes. With the advent of the *sarong kebaya*, Straits silversmiths quickly adapted to this change

Fig. 75 Here is an assortment of jade (Burmese green jadeite) and pearl jewellery, also from Penang, showing a rare three-piece *kerosang* set joined together by triple chains, a lovely pair of earrings, a pendant and a pair of bracelets. Mariette collection.

Fig. 76 The four pearl-studded brooches shown here are not *kerosang* brooches for securing the tunic-like *baju* or the *kebaya* blouse. They are brooches fashioned after the style of nineteenth-century Victorian jewellery. From Penang. Mariette collection.

Fig. 77 A set of the older variety of brooches (*kerosangs*) which, in the days gone by, were regularly used by nonyas wearing the typical *baju kurong*, i.e., a set of dress consisting of a long-sleeved tunic reaching to the knees and a batik *sarong*. The semi-precious, transparent stones (probably a variety of crude industrial diamonds) on the heart-shaped and circular brooches are mounted in box-settings. Silvergilt. Diameter of circlets: 3.7 cm. Length of large brooch: 7.5 cm. From Singapore. Mrs. Ho Wing Meng.

of fashion by creating a more up-to-date set of *kerosangs*, in keeping with the spirit of changing times.

The newer type of *kerosangs* also consists of three brooches except that they are all identically leaf-shaped, while the decorative design consists of a network of floral sprays executed in cut-through work and mounted either with pearls or precious and semi-precious stones in *à jour* setting to enhance the light-reflecting properties of those colourless transparent stones mined in Kalimantan, Indonesia. The *kerosangs* (see figs. 75 & 101) themselves are linked to each other by short, single or double chains. Since each of these brooches consists of a network of floral and foliated motifs, and since every individual leaf and flower is cut through to provide an opening for setting one of these transparent stones, the overall appearance presented by these *kerosangs* is a complex of glittering stones. *Kerosangs* of this type were particularly lovely when pinned on the

frontal hems of the *kebaya* dress. They can still be seen in the more antiquated goldsmith shops in Singapore and Penang, but the demand for them has dropped so drastically during the last few decades that entire rows of silversmiths along Arab Street and Jalan Sultan in Singapore closed shop many years ago.

The typical *kerosang* of older vintage is a flat, circular ring of about 3 cm in diameter on the average, and mounted on the obverse side with a single row of pearls or those 'swan p'ik' stones from Kalimantan by the age-old technique of box-setting (see figs. 77 & 79). Box-setting is a jeweller's technique of mounting jewels of great antiquity going back to ancient Egypt and possibly Mesopotamia about four thousand years ago, as jewellery recovered from the tombs of ancient pharaohs (e.g., the magnificent scarab pendant of Tutankhamen)[27] testify. These 'boxes' or frames for holding the gem in position consist of tiny, circular mountings, and are quite simply fashioned out of short, thin strips of gold or silver soldered on to the base plate of the *kerosang*.

Until the introduction of the relatively modern techniques of cutting gems to perfect geometrical shapes and facets such as the 'rose-cut', the 'table-cut', the 'step-cut', the 'star-cut' and the 'brilliant-cut', for example, ancient jewellers had to make do with misshapened gems of defective colours

Fig. 78 Here are three sets of the older variety of nonya *kerosangs* showing the typical combination of a heart-shaped (some say it is a peach-shaped) *kerosang* with two circular ones. All the stones are mounted in box-settings. Length of largest *kerosang* is 7 cm. From Malacca. Mrs. Ho Wing Meng and Mariette.

and grains by devising various methods of mounting gems with a view to show them off in the best possible light by concealing certain inherent flaws in them. Box-setting was effective in at least two different ways. Firstly, by applying a thin coating of dark gray or bluish enamel into the interior of the frames before inserting the stones, it was possible to correct defects due to cracks and impurities of colour by making the gems present a dark and uniform glow. Secondly, modifying the shapes of the frames holding the gems to make them look like rosettes or lozenges had the effect of correcting structural irregularities of the more misshapened gems.

Of course, where the types of stones employed were of a good colour and transparency, there was no necessity to seal up the sides and the bases of the gems, as this would hinder the natural beauty and fire of the gems in question. Jewellers therefore devised another technique of mounting jewels and this is known as *à jour* setting (see fig. 80). According to students of ancient jewellery this technique was introduced in Europe during the tenth century.

Quite simply, the technique of *à jour* setting consists of fashioning simple, ring-shaped frames

Fig. 79 Of the five heart-shaped *kerosangs* shown here, the top three pieces belong to
the commoner variety of brooches which may differ from one another only in minor
details, such as the kinds of semi-precious stones used, the quality of the gilding, or
perhaps minute details in the motifs. The two lower pieces of *kerosangs*, however,
depart quite significantly in the style of the design: instead of abstract patterns the
silversmith used organic motifs depicting flower buds, prawns and birds executed in
appliqué work. Average length: 6 cm. From Malacca. Author's collection.

Fig. 80 This set of *kerosangs* differs from the general run of the more archaic variety of nonya brooches. The rings in which the stones are embedded are hollow and the silversmith employed the technique of *à jour* mounting to take advantage of the greater transparency (and thus the great light-reflecting quality) of the stones. The overall effect is a richer and more glittering brooch. Greatest width: 5 cm. From Malacca. Mrs Ho Wing Meng.

of pre-determined sizes into which the gems may be tightly fitted along the thin outer edge, thus leaving both the upper and lower sides of the jewel open to allow light to pass through. However *à jour* settings by simple circular rings or claw-like clasps only became possible after lapidaries had developed various techniques of polishing and cutting diamonds and other precious stones. By the fifteenth and sixteenth centuries, European lapidary techniques had developed to the stage where the application of diamond and corundum dust for facet-cutting enabled gem-cutters (especially those of Antwerp and Amsterdam) to grind gems into cone-shaped stones with flat tops and pointed bases (octahedrons) for maximum reflection of light. Undoubtedly the development of improved techniques of cutting and faceting gems when combined with *à jour* setting produced a far more scintillating appearance in gemstones.

There are several variations in the method of *à jour* setting. The simplest is a ring-shaped frame, just described, into which the stone is first of all inserted and gradually secured together by the process of hammering the sides of the frame until it forms a tight collar around the gem. The second method is also similar to the first except that tiny granulations of silver (or gold) are soldered over the surrounding edges of the frame to provide, as it were, minute clasps to hold the stones in position. Besides serving a useful function, these tiny bits of granules also improve the general appearance of the decorative design. The third method dispenses with the use of frames by providing, instead, a circle of finger-like clasps to hold up the gem. The advantage of this technique is that it enables a jewel of flawless transparency and brilliance to be exhibited in the best possible light, especially when the clasps are so structured as to raise the stone well above the matrix of the general design. For diamonds and other types of solitaires, the finger-clasp mounting is preferable.

Fig. 81 Here are two sets of archaic nonya *kerosangs* executed entirely in granulé work and showing the Straits silversmith at his best in this technique of ornamentation. Brooches in granulation work are necessarily heavier and more solidly constructed. Silvergilt. Length of the largest brooch: 5 cm. From Singapore. Mrs. Ho Wing Meng.

Fig. 82 A set of *kerosangs* fabricated in a combination of pierced and granulé work. Notice, too, that the granulation blobs are not simple globular droplets, but rather granules specially faceted and polished to present a variety of reflecting planes. Diameter of star-shaped brooches: 4.5 cm. From Penang. Mariette collection.

One other method of embellishing brooches made to nonya tastes is that of granulation. Essentially this is done by applying little globules of molten silver of various sizes to the flat surface of the *kerosang* circlet. In the hands of a master craftsman, however, this simple method of ornamentation can be used with great effect to produce articles of attractive designs. Fig. 81 shows two sets of granulé-work *kerosangs*, each with two circlets designed somewhat after the shape of a floral garland. The third complementary brooch of each of these two sets of *kerosangs* is that of the finger citron. Notice here how the silversmith enhanced the ornamental works of the granulated surface of the circlet by (1) cutting and filing both the inner and outer edges of the plain ring till they 'bristle', as it were, with a delightful series of saw-like teeth of different sizes, and (2) with regard to the set in fig. 81 (left) as well as that shown in fig. 82, by faceting the various droplets of silver granules to present a multi-reflecting surface. The nett result is a *kerosang* set of very solid construction and distinctive design.

The method of faceting granulé brooches is quite simple: it consists of hammering the various globules of silver which have already been soldered on to the obverse surface of a flat circular ring. A tiny flat-tip puncher is used for this purpose. Now there is no doubt that faceted granulé work involves additional labour, and that in their original, polished conditions, brooches of this sort must have presented a scintillating appearance. Whether they were aesthetically more pleasing than the simpler granulé work consisting of tiny semi-hemispherical globules, is perhaps another matter – I prefer the style of granulé brooches shown in fig. 81 (right). But in the days gone by, *kerosangs* with faceted granulé designs must have appealed to a fair following of nonya clients. Be that as it may, *kerosangs* with granulé designs tended to be larger and heavier than the general run of stone-mounted brooches.

The simple, ring-shaped *kerosang* may be the oldest and most conservatively designed of nonya brooches. But as far as I have been able to ascertain, there is no reliable method to determine the age of a particular antique *kerosang*, because the inherent conservativism of Chinese art and craftsmanship required a particular artefact having a successful design to be produced endlessly without any change. Nevertheless contemporaneous with the simple ring-shaped *kerosang* is another one of formalized, heart-shaped design. Brooches of this variety are invariably mounted with pearls and 'swan p'ik' on the top surface after the ancient method of box-setting. In traditional Straits Chinese practice the heart-shaped *kerosang* was always matched with two ring-shaped ones. The average length of such brooches is 7.5 cm and the width is 4 cm though some exceptionally large *kerosangs* may exceed 9.5 cm long and 6.5 cm wide. And judging by some of the pre-1900 photographs of wealthy nonyas, Penang nonyas were particularly noted for their impressive, heart-shaped brooches (made of gold) which they proudly pinned to frontal hems of their *baju kurong* just below the neck, followed by two smaller circular brooches below.

It is difficult to say whether the heart-shaped *kerosang* was derived from a design of purely local origin, or else a copy of some old brooches of European origin. My own opinion is that this quaint-looking brooch was adapted from some long-forgotten brooches brought over from Britain, because some late seventeenth- or eighteenth-century Celtic brooches in the Museum of Scottish Antiquities in Edinburgh look very similar to these nonya *kerosangs*. Actually, circular brooches in which the sharp, pointed end of the movable pin is exposed on the top surface of the circlet are considerably older. They date back to the Middle Ages in Europe, when it was the custom of the monks to employ such brooches to secure their cloaks in position. As far as I know, the heart-shaped *kerosang* is not of Chinese or Hindu-Islamic origin. Judging from its close resemblance to the Celtic-styled Scottish brooch, we may presume that Straits Chinese silversmiths borrowed the general design of this brooch from some European archetypes brought to Malacca, either by the Portuguese, the Dutch or, as I believe it, by the British. As usual, local silversmiths modified the details of the decorative work by mounting the surface with rough-cut industrial diamonds, adding several appliqued motifs of birds and phoenixes and attaching a huge rosette to the top of the brooch.

The reader is well reminded that although all these nonya *kerosangs* present a pleasantly archaic appearance about them, they may at most be dated only as far back as the beginning of the nineteenth century. We have, as yet, no evidence, either direct or circumstantial, to prove the existence of such *kerosangs* dating back to the eighteenth or seventeenth century, though they surely must have existed, in one form or another, long before the British came to Malacca. After all the Chinese have been living in Malacca since the beginning of the fifteenth century. Even if we assume that the introduction of these heart-shaped *kerosangs* came with the Portuguese one hundred years later, we are still left with the anomalous position of not being able to establish the existence of these artefacts dating back to the Portuguese era. Archaelogical evidence may some day resolve the problem.

Fig. 83 Of the two Malay-styled hairpins shown here, the one on the right is more interesting as it is designed in the more conservative tradition. The semi-precious stones in unfaceted cabochon cuts are mounted in box-settings. Length: 13 cm. From Johore.

Hairpins

The rather long equivalent for hairpins in Baba Malay is instructive as it is interesting. Literally it means 'to pick the ear, to pierce through the hair' or, in other words, a hairpin which is designed in the shape of a gigantic ear-pick. As is probably well-known to many people, ear-picking has always been a popular toilet habit of the Chinese, and for this purpose they had devised since time immemorial a little metal stick made of silver, brass or gold, about 9 and 10 cm long, modified at one end into a tiny scoop. Now all nonya hairpins were described as *kerok kuping chuchuk sanggul*, or simply *sanggul chuchuk* for short, because (as the Malay name suggests) the original design of these hairpins must have been inspired by the shape of this humble instrument; in fact, even the most sophisticated design of nonya hairpins still retains the general form of the *kerok kuping* (see fig. 83).

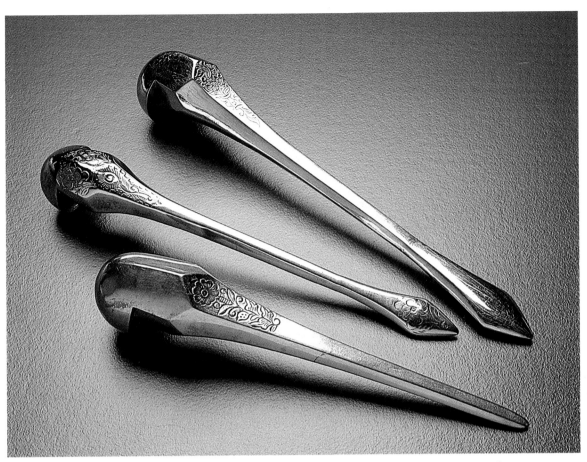

Fig. 84 A set of the more conservative type of hairpins worn by Singapore (and Malacca) nonyas of the pre-World War I generation. Up to the time of World War II, only nonyas sporting the *baju kurong* wore this type of hairpin. The design is bold and simple. Silvergilt. Lengths vary between 13 cm and 17 cm. From Singapore.

As in the case of the *kerosangs*, the Malacca and Singapore nonyas traditionally wore their hairpins in sets of three, although the Portuguese nonyas of Malacca who adopted the Malay *baju kurong* and Malay coiffure, were reputed to have stuck five pieces of hairpins into their hair-buns. Penang nonyas did even better: they wore six hairpins by sticking them into a semi-circular bun of hair just above their foreheads. Usually these hairpins rest on what appears to be a low semi-circular band of silver. When a Penang nonya decked her hair with six of these hairpins, she looked as if she were wearing a low tiara of some sort.

There are several types of nonya hairpins. The first and possibly the most conservative-looking of them (see fig. 84) is fashioned after the form of a huge ear-pick, one end of which is modified to look like a faceted bolt of some sort which gradually tapers to a point at the opposite extremity. The surface of the hairpin is plain except for a small patch of floral engravings on the crown. The rest is unadorned but polished to a mirror-like shine. The biggest of these hairpins looks formidably large and heavy. It is large as nonya hairpins go, but it is not heavy. This is because such hairpins are made of beaten silver and thus hollow inside. As far as one can make out, such hairpins were fabricated in two halves and then soldered together. But the absence of any seam lines gives these *kerok kuping* the impression of great sturdiness and solidity. It was customary to have all such hairpins gilded and polished. The largest of these hairpins measures up to 16 cm long, while the shortest of them average 12 cm in length. In the nonya style of hairdressing, the two larger hairpins are pierced cross-wise into the tightly-knotted hair-bun set well to the top of the head, while the third and shortest hairpin is inserted a little distance below the second hairpin. Hairpins of this type were confined to Singapore and Malacca nonyas.

A variation of the above type of *sanggul chuchuk*

Fig. 85 Two other variations of the so-called 'Portuguese hairpins' from Malacca. Notice that the 'crowns' are modelled after the shape of a cockle shell, while the only type of ornamentation permitted are the facetings on the upper portion of the stem. Silvergilt. Lengths vary between 9 cm and 12 cm.

is one which is smaller but literally fashioned like a ear-pick (see fig. 85). Here the crown of the hairpin is a hemispherical scoop with fluted designs on the outside to simulate the texture of a cockleshell. The long, tapering pin is practically chased throughout its entire length with lozenge facets to minimize the stark simplicity of the design. Although it has not been conclusively established, my own conjecture based upon a close examination of the structure and design of these hairpins is that they were always worn in sets of five rather than in sets of three. I am suggesting, in other words, that such hairpins were probably patronized largely by the Portuguese nonyas of Malacca.

The most ornate of nonya hairpins (see fig. 86) are those in which the typical ear-pick scoop or bolt-like crowns have been modified to form a spray of floral and foliated motifs executed in cut-through work for mounting gemstones of various sorts mounted in *à jour* settings and fine granules. Invariably the 'crown' of the floral spray curves inward to form a scoop typical of all nonya hairpins. Actually the crown of floral and foliated spray was separately crafted and mounted with gems before being soldered on to the tapering stem of the hairpin. Most of these hairpins measure about 11 cm long on the average. Pearls of the baroque variety with a yellowish lustre were often used on those hairpins intended for mourning, but 'swan p'ik' or industrial diamonds, emeralds and sapphires were also employed occasionally. Since both the pearls and gems used are of irregular shapes, Straits silversmiths devised an ingenious method of improving the general appearance of these hairpins by soldering tiny granules of silver over the edges of the floral and foliated frames in which the gemstones are embedded.

Fig. 86 These handsome pearl-studded hairpins with crowns of floral and foliated sprays and executed in pierced work have a distinctive nineteenth-century European look about them. I am inclined to think that these hairpins were unique to the Singapore nonyas, for I have rarely encountered them in Malacca. They are practically non-existent in Penang. Among the better pieces, the baroque pearls have a faintly yellowish lustre about them. Lengths vary between 10 cm and 13 cm. From Singapore. Mrs. Ho Wing Meng.

In fig. 87 we see some lovely and archaic-looking examples of the so-called 'Portuguese hairpins' used traditionally by Portuguese nonyas in Malacca. Incidentally, these hairpins are not of Portuguese origin in the sense that they originated from Portugal and were crafted by Portuguese jewellers. They were, in fact, made by Chinese silversmiths in Malacca as the stamped characters on the tapering stems of these hairpins indicate. The name 'Portuguese hairpins' merely implies that they were made specifically to Portuguese nonya tastes. Notice that in these hairpins Straits silversmiths used box-setting to mount the gemstones. The general design of the crown retains the traditional form of the ear-pick. Portuguese hairpins were generally longer then the general run of nonya hairpins – their average length being 13.5 cm.

Generally, nonya hairpins can be distinguished from those which were imported from China by their strict adherence to the basic design of the typical ear-pick. Why the Straits nonyas should have insisted that their hairpins retained the fundamental shape of the Chinese ear-pick is not at all clear to me. After all, there was nothing symbolically significant about the ear-pick in Chinese folklore. Indeed hairpins traditionally made in China came in a wide variety of shapes and sizes, but none of the extant pieces that I have seen was ever designed to look even remotely like a ear-pick. It could be that the ear-pick hairpin was not of Chinese origin. Could it then have been inspired by similar articles of old Javanese and Sumatran origins? This is possible, except that none of the old Indonesian hairpins which I have seen might plausibly be said to be precursors of Straits Chinese hairpins.

My own conjecture is that nonya hairpins were inspired by similar hairpins of European origins which had been brought over either by the Portuguese, the Dutch or, as I am inclined to think, by those English ladies who accompanied their husbands to Malacca and Singapore during the nineteenth century. The only trouble with this hypo-

Fig. 87 A set of five 'Portuguese hairpins' reputedly worn by the Portuguese nonyas of Malacca during the nineteenth century. Such hairpins were, however, not made by Portuguese silversmiths but by Chinese jewellers, as the stamped Chinese marks clearly indicate. The 'crowns' of these hairpins are more reminiscent of old Malay-styled hairpins than the Straits Chinese varieties. Silvergilt. Lengths between the shortest and the longest vary between 13.5 cm and 16.5 cm. From Malacca. Author's collection.

thesis is that hairpins do not appear to have been a common item of ladies' jewellery in England. It is true that ornamental hair-clips of various sorts exist. But hairpins modelled after the form of a giant ear-pick, or something resembling a ear-pick with a poniard-like tapering stem, were extraordinarily unusual. In fact the only possible type of European hairpins having a poniard shape was the Scottish Dirk pin of ancient Celtic origin. The Victorian version of the Scottish Dirk pin is essentially shaped like a slim dagger ornamented with agate, jasper and carnelian stones on the flat surface of the metal stem. One end of the pin, the crown, is mounted with a large disk-like or bolt-like piece of agate or carnelian, and the other end tapers down to a narrow dagger-like point. Whether the nonya hairpin was in fact inspired by the Scottish Dirk pin is not easy to tell. But it appears that the Dirk pin is the only hairpin which resembles the nonya hairpin in its overall design.

Although nonya hairpins can be distinguished from those which were made by silversmiths in China by their adherence to the basic design of the typical Chinese ear-pick, they were not the only types of hairpins made by local silversmiths. For the more conservative Chinese women of non-peranakan extraction, Straits silversmiths also fabricated hairpins of more traditional Chinese

Fig. 88 Here, by way of contrast, we show a selection of hairpins made locally for the more conservative, China-born women. Notice here that unlike the designs of nonya hairpins which were all variations of the ear-pick, there is no standard design for such traditional Chinese hairpins. The latter type is also significantly shorter. Length: approx. 7.5 cm. From Singapore.

tastes. Fig. 88 show examples of some. Notice here that the design is somewhat different: in particular, the pin is shorter and more functional looking, while the decorative crown consists of a plate of beaten silver, variously shaped and ornamented with repoussé, chased or even appliqué work. Fig 88, second from left, shows a hairpin with a butterfly motif interpreted in a rather formalized fashion. The interesting feature here is the presence of four little frogs, very delicately and realistically depicted on the wings of the butterfly.

Chains and necklaces

With regard to chains and necklaces traditionally patronised by the Straits nonyas, there are no specific characteristics which mark them out as typically Straits Chinese in taste and design. The general style in the designs of these artefacts is not of Chinese origin but probably derived from old Indo-European archetypes which may have reached Southeast Asia *via* the Middle Eastern countries, India and then Sumatra during the heyday of the Srivijaya and Majapahit

empires, from the eighth to the fourteenth centuries of the Christian Era. For example the design of the necklace shown in fig. 89 is very closely related to those used by ancient Minoans and Greeks before the fifth century B.C., except that careful inspection reveals that the two parallel chains of rosettes look more like plum blossoms than the formalized rosettes of a similar necklace found in Tarentum, Italy. The stylized buds which hang from the lower chain of rosettes are also modifications of ancient Greek motifs.

Similarly, the multi-chained necklace shown in fig. 58 with its parallel and non-parallel rows of interlocking rosettes, could very well have been worn by some ancient Mesopotamian, Persian or Indian lady, though as far as can be ascertained, this necklace was fabricated in Malaya by Chinese silversmiths during the nineteenth century. Nonetheless, necklaces of such foreign designs (see figs. 60 & 61) were regularly worn by Straits Chinese brides until about the turn of the present century, when the fashion changed more and more in favour of the single-chained necklace matched with a pendant of some kind.

The making of these elaborate necklaces must have consumed much time and labour: for example, putting together the ancient Greek-

Fig. 89 When this necklace was first shown to me by a jeweller in Malacca about twelve years ago, my first thought was, 'How did such a splendid ancient Greek necklace get to this part of the world?'' My jeweller assured me, however, that it was in fact a product of local Chinese silversmiths, and he pointed out that the double, parallel rows of florets represented prunus blossoms. But it was obvious that the inspiration behind this necklace was European in origin. Silvergilt. Length: 47 cm. From Malacca. Author's collection.

styled necklace shown in fig. 89 required 268 connecting rings, 90 plum blossom rosettes and 44 stylized 'buds'. Each and every one of these little items had to be crafted by hand. Similarly, the elaborate multi-chained necklace shown in fig. 58 required nearly 600 tiny circular rings, about 320 tiny rosettes, 7 large panels with filigree work and three small ones at the bottom, or a total of nearly 1000 separate hand-crafted parts!

Although appliqued and filigree work seldom occur in the decorative designs of Straits silverwork, they are not entirely absent. Some of the other types of archaic-looking necklaces which were made up of a series of rectangular panels connected by multiple chains, sported filigree work in the decorative motifs.

Fig. 90 A large pendant with matching rope-twist chain. The pendant, executed in a combination of pierced and repoussé work, depicts the figure of the Kuanyin or Goddess of Mercy, flanked on either side with a pair of phoenixes set amidst peony blossoms. The reverse side of this pendant depicts a vertical panel with characters identifying the figure of the Kuanyin and flanked by two dragons. A work of impressive craftsmanship. Silvergilt. Length of pendant: 7.8 cm. From Singapore. Mrs. Ho Wing Meng.

Pendants

The designs of Straits Chinese pendants were drawn from various sources such as archaic Chinese pendants, Indo-European pendants and old Indonesian brooches-cum-pendants. The Straits nonyas, however, did not take to pendants of the cameo type with intaglio designs carved on semi-precious stones such as agate, jasper, onyx, lapis-lazuli or mother-of-pearl. Neither did they take to wearing locket pendants of the sorts European ladies greatly prized, namely, little oval heart-shaped cases containing a lock of hair or a miniature portrait of some loved one.

The babas as well as the more conservative Chinese used to patronise a cylindrical type of locket as well as pendants with religious symbols (fig. 90) which, however, served as talismans or amulets rather than objects of sentimental value. The more traditional type of talismans worn by non-peranakan women and children were usually fabricated in the shape of a horizontal cylindrical box, or perhaps a formalized bat-shaped container with a detachable slot, to allow a small sheet of folded red paper (inscribed with Chinese characters purporting to be a prayer, a mantra or some mystical formulae written by a priest or a medium) to be inserted into the talisman container. It was believed that when such talismans

Fig. 91 This unique and fascinating pendant depicts a mud crab (modelled in the round) with two baby crabs (one of which is missing), each suspended from one claw. Hanging directly beneath the mandible region is a bunch of five keys signifying the Five Blessings, namely, longevity, riches, serenity, love of virtue and a crowning end to one's life. Length: 6 cm. From Singapore. Author's collection.

were worn around the neck, they helped to ward off evil, sickness and bad luck.

There are no pendants in extant which might be described as typically Straits Chinese in style, because the Straits nonyas wore a variety of pendants. Some were of archaic Chinese designs while others looked more like European pendants modified with local motifs of one sort or another (see fig. 92). However, pendants (see fig. 93) sporting floral and foliated motifs and studded with pearls or precious and semi-precious stones came closer to nonya tastes. These became popular with the nonyas from about the time of World War I (1914–18).

Fig. 92 Two necklaces with matching pendants: the upper chain in rope-twist design
has a medallion pendant of the type which was greatly popular with Malay clients, while
the lower chain sporting a *ch'i-ling* pendant was preferred by Chinese clients of more
traditional taste. Silvergilt. From Johore. Mrs. Ho Wing Meng.

Fig. 93 Penang nonyas were especially fond of pearl jewellery – more so than their counterparts in Malacca and Singapore. The three distinctive pendants shown here all came from Georgetown, Penang. Mrs. Ho Wing Meng and Mariette.

Fig. 94 Two types of earrings are shown in this picture: the three pairs of rather Oriental workmanship are typical of conservative Chinese earrings, while the two pairs on the right are obviously of Straits Chinese taste. In nonya earrings, one can detect the influence of ancient Greek or medieval European jewellery at work. From Singapore. Mrs. Ho Wing Meng and Mariette.

Fig. 95 Of the four different types of pearl-studded earrings shown here, the top three pairs are ear-studs. The beautiful pair of drop earrings on the left is exceptional even by Penang standards of elegance. Mariette et al.

Earrings and finger-rings

The designs of earrings and finger-rings (see fig. 94 & 95) are also largely interpreted in terms of floral or foliated motifs set with pearls and stones. For daily use the average nonyas seemed to have preferred simple studs, each of which was mounted with a single pearl, emerald or ruby. As it was the custom in those days for all women to have a little hole pierced through the lower lobe of each ear so that they could wear earrings, all such ornaments of vintage design have no clips on them. They must be secured to the ears by various inverted hook-like devices for insertion into tiny ear-holes. Antique ear-studs are secured by screws and other decorative bolts. On formal occasions, however, it was proper for the nonyas to wear drop earrings.

Fig. 96 Here is an assortment of traditional Straits Chinese bracelets (usually gilded unless intended for mourning or burial purposes) sporting the typical spiral- or barley-twist design. Variations of the simple spiral-twist abound, and here we show five different types. The bracelet on the bottom is an exceptional piece of craftsmanship. From Singapore. Mrs. Ho Wing Meng and Mariette.

Finger-rings always came in pairs and must be worn in pairs. Invariably they were worn on the third and fourth fingers. On this point, it should be noted that the Straits nonyas, unlike aristocratic Chinese ladies in China, did not prize green jade as the most desirable of precious stones. Jade, therefore, rarely features among the precious stones used in Straits Chinese jewellery except in ornaments made for the Penang nonyas. In fact, the nonyas preferred emeralds with their scintillating fire to Burmese jadeite.

Bracelets and anklets

Until about the turn of the present century, according to a number of nonyas whom I consulted, the most popular type of Straits Chinese bracelet was a simple arm circlet made of three, five or seven solid cords of silver (or gold) twisted in rope-like fashion. The simplest and probably the oldest version of the rope-twist bracelet was a twisted cord cut to a specific length and then bent in the form of a circlet until the two ends meet. The making of such bracelets by twisting various solid strands of silver cords into a rope-like appearance was intended not only to give an ornamental effect, but also to confer a certain tension which enables the bent circlet to preserve its integrity of form by resisting any force to pull it apart. A bracelet of this sort can be worn around the wrist either by slipping it through the hand or by prising the two unattached ends apart and then slipping it sideways into the wrist.

In fig. 96 we illustrate five different types of nonya bracelets featuring the characteristic spiral-twist or 'barley-twist' styles. The pair of bracelets on the top left is fabricated out of three strands of silver cords, while the topmost pair is made up of seven strands of silver cords wound around a central core of solid silver cord. It appears that the greater the number of strands employed in the

Fig. 97 Two pairs of Straits Chinese anklets in different designs. They are made of beaten silver and are hollow inside. The pair on the right is plain and virtually unadorned except for two decorative knobs joining the two ends together. The pair on the left however is designed after the fashion of bamboo stems and Buddha finger citrons. Silvergilt. Diameter: 9.5 cm. From Singapore.

fabrication of these bracelets, the greater was the structural tension preserving them. Of the remaining three varieties of spiral-twist bracelets shown in fig. 96, the lower piece features a more complicated and interesting style of rope-twist design. This delightful and rather ingenious piece of craftsmanship was achieved quite simply by fashioning, in the first instance, three separate lengths of double-stranded silver cords lightly wound together. Next these three double-stranded lengths of silver cords were then brought together and wound to form a complex of twisted cords. The two ends were then trimmed and soldered, each with a small, circular disc, to prevent the various rope strands from coming a-part under their outward springing tension. Final-ly, this compound length of rope-twists was bent to form a typical bracelet.

Since a rope-twist bracelet preserves its integrity of form mainly by the tension under which

the various cords are maintained, the wear and tear which it is subjected to over a long period of time, especially by the need to pull apart the two unattached ends, would eventually cause it to lose its state of tension and become distorted in shape. To overcome this difficulty, Straits silversmiths, designed an improved version of the rope-twist bracelet. This is done by dividing the entire length of the compound rope-twists into two equal and separate semi-circular parts and joining the two semi-circular parts by hinges at one end and screw and bolt at the other end. To wear a bracelet of this form, one no longer needs to prise apart the two unjointed ends. All that needs to be done is to unwind the screw at one end until the two seg-ments come apart.

Not all rope-twist bracelets found in Malaysia are of Chinese origin; some are the products of by-gone Malay silversmiths. Generally speaking, Chinese bracelets are heavier, being made of

Fig. 98 This unusual pair of bracelets with figures carved into the central panels is, of course, uncharacteristic of Straits silverwork. In fact it is a product of South China silversmiths in Amoy as the characters stamped on the reverse side indicate. Silvergilt. Diameter: 7 cm. Mrs. Ho Wing Meng.

solid, twisted cords of silver, and in most cases, stamped with Chinese characters giving the shop-names and/or indicating the nature of the metal. Most spiral-twist bracelets of Malay workmanship are made of beaten silver and hence hollow inside. The rope-twist design is merely a simulation of the actual process of rope-twisting techniques employed in Chinese bracelets. Besides, the Malay version of the rope-twist bracelet is not fashioned out of two equal, semi-circular segments joined end-to-end. On the contrary, one of these segments was made much longer than the other, so that the two semi-circular segments overlapped. The result is a circlet of unsymmetrical design. The pair of bracelets on the right of fig. 96 has a simulated spiral-twist design. It is hollow inside and is of Chinese workmanship.

The pair of bracelets or anklets (and the distinction between a bracelet and an anklet is not all that clear-cut) on the top left of fig. 97 is perhaps of more conservative Chinese design. It is made of beaten silver and is fabricated out of two equal, semi-circular segments joined by hinges and screw. The two segments are designed after the manner of bamboos but terminating with a Hand-of-Buddha, or finger citron, on each end.

If the above-mentioned bracelets are representative samples of Straits Chinese designs, then it would come as no surprise if students attribute the two pairs of circlets shown in fig. 98 to the handi-work of mainland Chinese silversmiths. The style is distinctly foreign to locally-made silver brace-lets: for example, the central band of decorative motifs consisting mainly of figures and animals does not appear to have been executed by the technique of repoussé punching. The sharp and solid reliefs suggest that they had been carved out of a solid sheet of silver. The method of gilding is

also unusual. Instead of fire-gilding by painting a coat of mercury in which pure gold has been dis-solved in it and then heated to drive away the mer-cury, gold foils were applied cold on to the silver base. The flakings of the foils indicate this. In fact this pair of bracelets is from Amoy, South China, as the two characters 'Hsia Mên' (厦门) stamped on the inside band suggest. Several other stamped characters give the shop or goldsmith's name, as 'Kim Chien Huat' (金建发), while the characters 'Chia Yung' (家用) intimate that these bracelets had originally been commissioned for a particular family.

Chinese bracelets are always made in pairs or multiples of two, and in the days gone by, it was customary for a woman to wear one bracelet on each wrist. The same goes for anklets which are basically nothing more than larger versions of the arm circlet, except that Straits Chinese anklets were largely modelled after those of Hindu-Malay archetypes. In ancient China it was not customary for women to wear anklets. This was a practice which the native Malays originally borrowed from the Indians. Fig. 99 shows some of these Hindu-Islamic anklets found in Malaya. How-ever, most antique dealers and jewellers in Johore and Malacca were unanimous in attributing these anklets to the products of a bygone breed of Straits silversmiths. They were said to have been made exclusively for Malay clients.

Except in South Thailand (e.g. Surathani and Pattani) and parts of Peninsular Malaysia where anklets of this type are still being worn by women during weddings, or other religious and ceremo-nial occasions, most often Malay women, like their counterparts in the Straits Chinese com-munity, ceased wearing such anklets more than half a century ago.

Fig. 99 The three pairs of anklets shown here are, of course, the products of local Chinese silversmiths, as the stamped Chinese characters on the lower anklets indicate. But these ornaments were actually intended for Malay and Southern Thai clients. They are large anklets (diameter averaging 12 cm!) and the formalized ornamental motifs were clearly made to suit Islamic taste. All the anklets are hollow inside. Silvergilt. From Malacca. Mrs. Ho Wing Meng.

Fig. 100 This pair of broad-band bracelets sporting formalized appliqué floral motifs and overlapping bands soldered side by side, was not used by the Straits nonyas. Bracelets of this sort, once frequently encountered in the State of Johore, were made by Chinese silversmiths for Malay clients. From Johore.

Pearl ornaments

Most extant pieces of pearl ornaments and jewellery shown in figs. 75, 76, 93, 95 & 101, excepting those pearl-studded hairpins sporting a spray of leaves or lotus blossoms, and which are unique to the Singapore and Malacca nonyas (see fig. 86) , came from the private collections of Penang nonyas. They are rarely encountered either in antique shops or in baba family heirlooms in Malacca and Singapore; so it may be presumed that pearl-studded ornaments and jewellery were not particularly fashionable with the nonyas of Malacca and Singapore.

Even the most flawless of pearls lack the sparkle and inner fire which diamonds, emeralds, rubies and blue sapphire emit. At their best, pearls are merely lustrous with a slight tinge of yellow about them. But what made pearl ornaments unsuitable for use on ceremonial occasions is the fact that pearls are largely white – the colour of mourning, according to old Chinese customs. For this reason, perhaps, the nonyas of Malacca and Singapore generally avoided pearls, except when obliged to use them in times of mourning. But even so extant samples of pearl-studded jewellery are few and far between – the explanation for this being that other substitutes for pearl-studded jewellery were available, namely, ungilded silver artefacts left in their pristine whiteness. Until about ten or fifteen years ago, old silversmiths in various parts of Singapore, Johore and Malacca regularly maintained small stocks of silver jewellery and ornaments intended for use during mourning.

The nonyas of Penang, however, took a great liking to pearl ornaments and jewellery, for they appreciated the quiet lustre and subdued colours of pearls especially when used in combination with green Burmese jades. This is clearly borne out by the fact that pearl ornaments and jewellery are more frequently seen in private collections there than in Malacca and Singapore. The designs of most of these pearl ornaments which include pendants, brooches, earrings, finger-rings, *kerosangs* and bracelets are largely European in taste, though some of the motifs, among them dragonflies, cicadas and butterflies, are clearly of Chinese origin. Occasionally, one encounters a brooch or a pendant which is fashioned in the form of a star or a crescent moon with several stars inside the arc – shapes reminiscent of Islamic taste.

The more perceptive student of Straits silver will have noticed that the silver *frameworks* for these pearl-and-jade variety of Penang-styled ornaments are never gilded. Whether its significance is related to traditional Chinese religious practices, or whether it was dictated by the accepted notions of good taste of the time, is not really clear. In any case, if the reader would take the trouble to consult extant photographic portraits of Penang nonyas at about the turn of the present century, and look carefully at the kind of jewellery they wore, he will notice that such pearl, or pearl-and-jade ornaments, were regularly used.

Fig. 101 Except for the three-piece, leaf-shaped *kerosangs* in the picture, all the rest of the articles are pearl bracelets. *Kerosangs* in leaf-shape and connected by chains are said to have come from Sumatra, probably Medan, and gained popularity with nonyas from about the time of the First World War (1914–18). From Penang. Mariette collection.

As for the kind of pearls used in these articles, they belong to the Oriental baroque variety, that is to say, natural pearls of somewhat irregular shapes and very lightly tinged with a yellowish lustre. Others of a lesser quality tend to have a grayish cast about them. Most of these antique pieces of pearl-studded ornaments as we find them today have a dull and faded appearance. This is because these articles have not been used for a long time, and with pearls, the lustrous gleam of the surface nacre decays with passing time. A light acid treatment could, however, restore these gems back to their pristine glories.

In practically every one of these pearl-studded ornaments, the individual motifs are executed in pierced work and suitable hollows are then cut through to contain pearls of various shapes and sizes. As a rule, Straits Chinese silversmiths tried to minimize the inherent deficiencies of baroque pearls by enclosing them within the formalized patterns of flower petals or leaf-blades, and also by the applications of tiny droplets of silver soldered to the sides of the various pearls. The nett effect is that the structural deficiencies in these pearls are more or less covered up. Thus, despite their misshapened proportions, baroque pearls in Straits Chinese jewellery are made to blend harmoniously with the archaic designs of these articles.

I should like to conclude this section on Straits Chinese jewellery with a description of the legendary wealth of rich peranakan Chinese in Malacca during the latter part of the nineteenth century. The following quotation is taken from Isabella L.

Bird's well-known book *The Golden Chersonese (and the Way Thither)* published in 1883 by John Murray. Miss Bird (later Mrs. Bishop) was in Malacca in 1879 during the Chinese New Year celebrations, and a certain Mrs. Shaw, with whom she was staying at the time, was visited by four Chinese children (obviously from a wealthy merchant family) who were decked in their finest New Year clothes. This is what Miss Bird saw:

'During the morning, four children of a rich Chinese merchant attended by a train of Chinese and Malay servants came to see Mrs. Shaw. There were a boy and a girl of five and six years old, and two younger children. A literal description of their appearance reads like fiction. The girl wore a yellow petticoat of treble satin (mandarin yellow) with broad box pleats in front and behind, exquisitely embroidered with flowers in shades of blue silk, with narrow box pleats between, with a trail of blue flowers on each. Over this there was a short robe of crimson brocaded silk, with a broad border of cream white satin with the same exquisite floral embroidery in shades of blue silk. Above this was a tippet of three rows of embroidered lozenge shaped "tabs" of satin. *The child wore a crown on her head, the basis of which was black velvet. At the top was an aigrette of diamonds of the purest water, the centre was as large as a six penny piece. Solitaires flashing blue flames blazed all over the cap, and the front was ornamented with a dragon in fine filigree work in red Malay gold set with diamonds. I fear to be thought guilty of exaggeration when I write that this child wore seven necklaces, all of gorgeous beauty. The stones were all cut in facets at the back and highly polished, and their beauty was enhanced by the good taste and skilful workmanship of the setting. The first necklace was of diamonds set as roses and crescents, some of them very large and all of great brilliancy; the second of emeralds, a few were as large as acorns, but spoilt by being pierced; the third of pearls set whole; and the fourth of hollow filigree beads in red, burnt gold; the fifth of sapphires and diamonds, the sixth a number of finely worked chains of gold with a pendant of gold filigree fish set with diamonds; the seventh, what they all wore, a massive gold chain, which looked heavy enough by itself to weigh down the fragile little wearer, from which suspended a gold shield, on which Chinese characters forming the child's name were raised in rubies, with fishes and flowers in diamonds round it, and at the same back a god in rubies similarly surrounded. Magnificent diamond earrings and heavy gold bracelets completed the display* (italics mine).

All this weight of splendour, valued at the very least at $40,000.00 was carried by a frail human mite barely four feet high, with a powdered face, a gentle, pensive expression and quiet grace of manner, who came forward and most winsomely shook hands with us, as with all the other grave, gentle mites . . .'[28]

WEDDING UTENSILS

Betel-nut or *sireh* boxes

Among the various communities of immigrant Chinese who came to settle in Malaya and Singapore during the last two hundred years or more, the peranakan Chinese were alone in having adopted the ancient Hindu-Malay custom

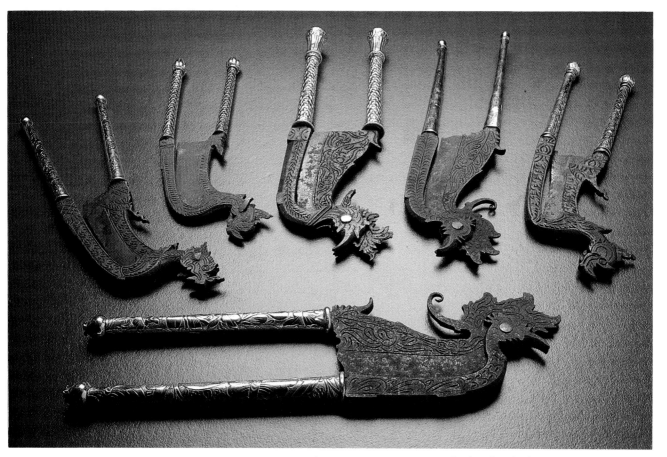

Fig. 102 Here is a selection of six betel-nut cutters which are usually found in Straits Chinese *sireh* sets. The cutters themselves are made of iron and designed after the manner of a formalized garuda bird. The handles are invariably sheathed in silver plate. Length of the largest cutter: 15 cm.

of chewing *sireh* leaves with slivers of betel nut, lime and gambier. To this end the wealthy Straits Chinese merchants and traders commissioned Straits silversmiths to turn out some very lovely objects of *virtu* in the shapes of little globular betel-nut boxes and cups of typically Straits Chinese taste.

Basically, a *sireh* set or *tempat sireh* consists of a lidless rectangular box which may be made of brass, lacquer-over-woodbase, blackwood inlaid with mother-of-pearl, namwood with gilt carvings, solid silver or even, in unusual instances, tortoise-shell, measuring about 25 cm long, 12.5 cm wide, and 6.25 to 12.5 cm high. The inside of the box is divided into two main compartments, one of which is rectangular and the other L-shaped. The rectangular partition is normally used to hold a pair of iron shears used for slicing betel nuts, while the L-shaped compartment holds two small globular covered boxes, a little cylindrical container for lime and a cup. In one of the

covered boxes shredded tobacco is kept, while the other may be used for keeping sliced betel nut or gambier and cloves. The gambier and cloves may sometimes be kept in the cup. Immediately below the top compartments is a 'concealed' drawer (it is concealed because casual glance may not reveal its presence) which was customarily used to hold the *sireh* leaves. The Malays and Thai Muslims of Surathani and Pattani kept their *sireh* leaves in a separate container of a modified pentagonal form called *bekas sireh*. Several examples of *bekas sireh* may be seen in Ling Roth's book, *Oriental Silverwork*.

Since it is cumbersome to have to carry a whole *sireh* set when one is travelling light, both the Malays and Thais (this is also true of the Malays in Brunei) devised several types of circular boxes for holding tobacco and sliced areca nuts. Such boxes are hung from chains which can be secured to the belt. The *chimbul* box for holding sliced betel nuts and the *chelpa* or tobacco box, are both of similar design, and they are among the most delightful of Malay *sireh* artefacts. Using the *chelpa* as a typical example, we note that it comes in a variety of shapes, including compressed spherical boxes, lobed boxes and octagonal boxes which are elaborately ornamented with chased and embossed designs. The babas did not, as a rule, carry separate tobacco and betel-nut containers as parts of their personal outfit, but nonetheless some beautiful examples of *chelpa* and *chimbul* boxes were turned out by Malay silversmiths for their nobility (see fig. 103).

Not all *sireh* sets made for the peranakan Chinese came in the shape of the typical rectangular *tempat sireh*; some in fact were made in the shape of a cylindrical lacquer box fashioned after the style of Burmese *sireh* sets. In the crafting of *sireh* sets intended for the Penang babas, we detect a variety of cultural influences at work, such as Burmese influence (circular lacquer boxes), Sumatran influence (pyramid-like rectangular lacquer boxes), and Malay-Thai influence (circular *tempat sireh*). Nevertheless, whatever the variations in the designs of *sireh* sets, those which are attributable to the handiwork of Straits silversmiths are quite easily recognizable by the types of the decorative motifs which ornamented these articles. As noted previously, Chinese workmanship invariably comes with such traditional art and auspicious symbols such as figures of Taoist immortals, dragons, *ch'i-lings*, phoenixes, and the flowers of the four seasons, while those of Malay origin have more restrained floral and foliated patterns.

There is much evidence, judging by the beauti-

ful workmanship and distinctive designs of those fine extant examples of *sireh* boxes in private collections, that Straits silversmiths expended much skill and patience in fabricating these humble, utilitarian objects of everyday use. The wealthier of Straits Chinese merchants and traders were so impressed with the craftsmanship of these early silversmiths that they made it a tradition to commission specially crafted *sireh* sets made to their tastes, so that these objects of *virtu* could be presented to the bride and groom at wedding ceremonies. Such *sireh* sets eventually became treasured family heirlooms as they were passed down from one generation to another.

The four *sireh* containers shown in fig. 104 were originally found without their accompanying *tempat sireh*. They were originally salvaged from an old, disused drawer of a cabinet containing all sorts of useless *bric-à-brac*. But because they had been so blackened with age, the real beauty of their chased designs did not become apparent until they had been cleaned and polished. The ornamental designs of these *sireh* containers are somewhat unusual as far as Straits silverwork go: they are executed entirely in chased work, and more importantly, in a style very reminiscent of T'ang period silverwork. This is particularly evident from the decorative designs of the hemispherical cover which depict boldly articulated sprays of floral scrolls with butterflies hovering among the foliage set against a finely dotted background. The designs on the lower half of the box are also T'ang-like in style; they depict a grapevine and twining branches weighed down with clusters of grapes and fat, bushy-tailed squirrels

Fig. 103 The three distinctive types of tobacco boxes shown here, and known as *chelpa* in Malay, are of Malay origin. In Straits Chinese customs, tobacco boxes were not made to be carried separately as in the case of the *chelpa* shown here: they were usually kept in one of those casket-like containers in the standard *sireh* set (see figs. 104–111). The largest box here measures 9 cm across. From Malacca, Mariette collection.

Fig. 104 A *sireh* set with the typical red lacquer box and the usual complements of *sireh* boxes and cups and a pair of shears for cutting areca nuts. The original owner must have treasured this set greatly, for she took the trouble to embroider two beaded panels for the inside of the *tempat sireh*. The lovely chased motifs on the caskets and cups have to be seen at close quarters to be appreciated. From Singapore. Author's collection.

Fig. 105 A *sireh* set very similar in design with that in fig. 107, the only difference being the *tempat sireh* here which is made of reddish lacquer painted with figure motifs. The caskets and cups, in silvergilt, are ornamented with fine, chased motifs which are reminiscent of T'ang period silverwork. From Singapore. Mrs. Ho Wing Meng.

Fig. 106 This is one of the smallest and simplest of *sireh* sets I have seen in many years. But it is by no means a toy of some kind: every article in the set is functional. The silver artefacts are finely chased with floral and foliated motifs set against a dotted ground. From Penang. Mariette collection.

Fig. 107 A *sireh* set sporting an unusual *tempat sireh* (the lidless rectangular box) of tortoise-shell and silver ormolu work. The globular caskets and cups are ornamented with fine chased motifs set against a dotted background. The style of the workmanship is similar to that of the *sireh* set in fig. 105. From Penang. Mariette collection.

scampering among the vines. The background is chased with little dots to give it a rich, matted appearance.

Among the varied repertory of artefacts made by silversmiths in China during the T'ang Dynasty, there were, however, no such things as *sireh* boxes. Nor were such articles ever crafted in China for export to Southeast Asia. The perpetuation of the T'ang period style of workmanship as seen in these *sireh* boxes (see figs. 105–107) could be attributed to the conservative habit of Chinese craftsmen to emulate a well-known art form for centuries on end. There is a box in the Carl Kempe Collection which is executed in similar chased work and motifs typical of the T'ang period. But it is given an eighteenth-century attribution. By parity of reasoning, it could be argued that Straits silverwork displaying such stylistic affinities should also be dated back to the eighteenth century. Unfortunately, there is no independent evidence to substantiate this claim, even though we know for a fact that the habit of chewing *sireh* leaves which the Straits babas adopted pre-dated the nineteenth century. Thus, apart from the style of the decorative designs, there is something about

the simple elegance of these *sireh* containers which suggests that they could have been early works of Straits silversmiths.

In figs. 104–112 we illustrate what is probably the finest selection of Straits Chinese *sireh* sets to be seen anywhere. Needless to say these treasured heirlooms had been acquired with considerable difficulty and only through the persistent efforts of several collectors during the course of the last ten years. A careful study of the various illustrations will show quite clearly how much skill and loving care the former generations of Straits silversmiths had invested in their handiwork. And when we consider how much of Straits silverwork has disappeared during the course of the last eighty years or so through the vicissitudes of the times, and especially through the depredations of the last Great War, we come to realize that the trouble which their various owners had taken to preserve these artefacts, betokens not only the sentimental value attached to these mementos of an affluent society, but also the artistic and possible investment values they represented. To the former generations of wealthy baba-nonyas, those *sireh* sets were vivid souvenirs of a bygone

Fig. 108 The *sireh* set shown here is of particular interest from an aesthetic point of view: the solid silver *tempat sireh* of unadorned simplicity and elegance is matched against a set of *sireh* boxes and cups of complex lobed bodies and ornate repoussé motifs and ormolu work. The weight of the silver box exceeds 1000 gm. From Singapore. Author's collection.

Fig. 109 A *sireh* set of luxurious design: the *tempat sireh,* fabricated out of solid silver panels, is ornately embossed on all the four side panels with phoenixes and floral motifs. Notice that there are *five* instead of the standard *four* caskets and cups – one of the covered boxes would most probably be used for holding tobacco. The areca-nut cutter in the set differs from the standard scissor-like shears; it consists of a metal cylinder and a chisel with a curved cutting edge. Mariette collection.

Fig. 110 In this picture we show a *sireh* set complete with all the essential ingredients for making *sireh* leaves, including that exceptional piece of accessory, the *anak lesong* or miniature pestle and mortar. The silver artefacts themselves are of high quality workmanship, as the cover of a casket shown in the foreground will indicate. Mariette collection.

Fig. 111 This lovely *sireh* set is remarkable not only for its attractive silver containers, but also for the fact that it incorporates a *bekas sireh* (i.e., *sireh* leaf container) on the lower left and a pair of shears fashioned after a horse rather than the usual garuda motif. The rectangular box made of heavy purple sandalwood is inlaid with coarse mother-of-pearl designs. From Penang. Mariette collection.

age of pomp and pageantry; to our eyes, perhaps, they offer glimpses of old-world splendour.

I have been assured by the various owners that these *sireh* sets once belonged to the estates of some of the wealthiest peranakan families in Singapore, Malacca and Penang. The various components of these remarkable *sireh* sets, particularly those globular, cylindrical and cup-like containers, are so consummately crafted that a cursory inspection will be sufficient to reveal the superb quality of the workmanship. Even the choice of materials that went into the making of those tapering *tempat sireh* was unusual: it included tortoise-shell embellished with silver ormolu work, beaten silver, purple sandalwood inlaid with mother-of-pearl designs, elephant ivory and ebony. As for the techniques of ornamentation employed, these included all the standard procedures known to silversmiths everywhere, namely, engraving, chased, repoussé, appliqué and even carved work. Sometimes gold ormolu work was added to enhance that sense of luxury. One areca-nut cutter had handles sheathed in gold, while the rest were covered with silver sheets. Fig. 19 shows a particularly remarkable *sireh* set of unusual craftsmanship.

I should like to add, as a tailpiece to this descriptive account of betel-nut boxes, a little anecdote concerning the cultural significance of the *tempat sireh* in Straits customs. While it is true that the presentation of *sireh* sets during traditional weddings was ostensibly intended to facilitate the enjoyment of chewing *sireh* leaves, the *sireh* set itself had a more serious and ominous function to fulfil in peranakan wedding customs. Several of the more knowledgeable babas intimated that in the days gone by, it was the privilege of the groom, if for some reason or other he was deeply unhappy with his bride (e.g., if he suspected, or had reason to believe, that she was unchaste), to signal his desire to annul the marriage by simply overturning the *tempat sireh* on his wedding bed.

My informants did not, however, say if they had known of actual instances in the past where this custom was put to the test, and what the consequences had been for both the bride's and the groom's families. Since marriages in the past had always been arranged by the elders, one would imagine that instances of weddings which had been annulled by the act of overturning a *tempat sireh* must have been extremely rare, if for no other reason than that elders who had been responsible for bringing their sons and daughters into wedlock would have tried to cover up such embarrassing scandals. Besides, it would take a headstrong and very independent groom to defy the niceties of customs and sensitivities by boldly overturning a *tempat sireh*, even if he had reason to believe that his bride was not a virgin. Since the peranakans have always been noted for their sense of courtesy and good manners, the majority of young and timid grooms who looked more like *gong kiah sie* (i.e., 'confused bridegrooms') than crafty crooks wise in the ways of the world could not be expected to act so brazenly as to overturn the *tempat sireh*. Nonetheless this was a privilege hallowed by ancient customs. So much then for male chauvinism!

Fig. 112 A splendid *sireh* set from a family heirloom in Penang. This is a paradigm case of masterly craftsmanship and sheer ornateness after the manner of Islamic art. The circular *tempat sireh* looks more like a tray than the standard rectangular box of the Malacca-Singapore variety. Although the design of the *sireh* set is purely Islamic in taste, the workmanship is Chinese – the chrysanthemums, prunus and bamboo motifs being clearly recognizable. Diameter of tray: 20 cm. Silvergilt. Mariette collection.

Plates and bowls

Even in the best of times, the wealthy and anglicized Straits Chinese did not attempt to imitate the European fondness for silverwares as status symbols to the point of commissioning some local or foreign silversmith to craft large platters, plates, dishes and bowls of every sort for use on banquets and other ceremonial occasions. They preferred *porcelain* wares, partly because the use of porcelain had always been a Chinese tradition even with the imperial court in Peking, and partly because there were certain intrinsic qualities about porcelain wares which made them superior to silver utensils. For example, porcelain articles are not affected by ugly tarnishes with the passage of time; the enamelled or glazed surface of porcelain wares does not react chemically when it comes into contact with food and beverages of every kind. For this reason, porcelain articles preserve the natural flavours of food much better than silver utensils. It is true that porcelains are brittle and may be chipped, cracked or even broken to pieces if they are not handled with care, but they do not become blackened, dented and misshapened by constant use.

This is not to say, however, that silver plates, dishes and bowls are entirely absent in the whole inventory of Straits Chinese silver. One does, in fact, encounter some small plates, dishes and bowls in family heirlooms of the more wealthy Straits Chinese families from time to time; and by all accounts available, most of the silver plates and dishes were used for making religious offerings. There is no evidence that rich Straits Chinese merchants and entrepreneurs made it a habit of commissioning specially inscribed silver plates

Fig. 113 This magnificent bowl showing two ferocious-looking dragons (executed in repoussé work), chasing after the fabled pearl amidst clouds and smoke, is not a product of Straits silversmiths, although it originally came from a baba home. It was probably presented as a gift to the owner by his business associates, and was obviously intended for the display cabinet rather than for some utilitarian purpose. No mark except for the number '90' stamped on the base. Diameter: 15 cm. From Singapore. Mrs. Ho Wing Meng.

and dishes to be given away as trophies. Neither did the Straits Chinese order silver shields, plaques, cups and medals to be given away on red-letter days. There were other ways of commemorating important and auspicious occasions, and these include the making of gifts of gold and silver jewellery and articles of *virtu*, specially designed polychrome enamelled wares, expensive embroidered costumes, feasting and dancing.

Following the practice of the British colonial officials of those times, some commemorative *bowls* (see figs. 113, 114 & 115) may have been presented to friends and valued business associates. But those uninscribed bowls could be no more than luxury articles intended to grace some display cabinets. By and large a typical Straits Chinese dinner service, consisting largely of plates, dishes and bowls of different sizes, was made of *porcelain* rather than silver. As I have described in another work,[29] the kind of porcelain utensils which the peranakan Chinese commissioned for their private use is a special type of polychrome wares known as Straits Chinese porcelain.

Thus, while porcelain bowls, cups, saucers, plates, jars and other kitchen utensils were among the commonest items of the kitchen and dining room cabinets, similar articles made of silver were exceptionally rare by comparison. As a matter of fact, I have not encountered more than a dozen pieces of plates and bowls in peranakan homes during the last ten years or so. The few pieces that came to light from time to time were mostly of South China provenance; the tell-tale marks of stamped English numerals such as '80' or '90' together with the presence of initials in English

Fig. 114 Here is another bowl from a baba heirloom in Singapore. The outside is quite plain except for a bold appliqué dragon hugging the sides. On the back are engraved the following words: 'Tan Boon Hong. For many distinguished services rendered. W.J. Napier.' The identity of W.J. Napier appears to present some difficulty, because there were several British figures in Singapore (and one in Hong Kong) during the 19th century whose 'Napier' was prefixed by 'W.J.' and 'W'. There was a William John Napier who died in Hong Kong in 1834. Diameter: 17 cm.
Mrs. Ho Wing Meng.

Fig. 115 This steep-walled, eight-lobed bowl is a product of some Shanghai silversmith — so it is marked. The designs, consisting of four principal motifs, namely, peonies, lotuses, bamboos and dragons, are depicted in pairs of identical panels placed diametrically opposite one another. The workmanship is fine and the motifs are neatly and clearly articulated in repoussé work. Silver bowls of this type had no functional value; they were bought or given away as trophies or mementos of some sort. Diameter: 13.5 cm. From Singapore. Author's collection.

Fig. 116 This bowl-like receptacle done in pierced work and depicting two dragons pursuing the legendary pearl, was probably intended to hold an ornamental glass bowl of some sort. It is obviously an example of nineteenth-century Chinese trade silver made for European markets. The workmanship is very similar to that of the bowl in fig. 113. Diameter: 15 cm. From Singapore.

Fig. 117 Silver plate finely engraved with a pair of phoenixes set amidst peony blossoms in a broad circular panel surrounding a central medallion depicted with a single peony blossom. The outer border is filled with the usual *pa chi hsiang* or eight happy omens interspersed at regular intervals with peonies. The style of this decoration is almost identical with the design of a variety of white-ground Straits Chinese porcelain plates and bowls originally made for the Tan Kim Seng family and marked 'Ta Ching Tao Kuan Yu Chih'. Diameter: 20 cm. From Malacca. Mariette collection.

alphabets on the bases of these articles, clearly indicate that these utensils had been crafted in Hong Kong, Canton or even Shanghai.

The ornamental receptacle (see fig. 116) with pierced work depicting dragons and clouds is a good example of old Hong Kong craftsmanship. Another smaller lobed bowl (see fig. 115) with steep sides and ornamented with dragons, bamboos and peonies duplicated in diametrically opposite panels and executed in repoussé work, is another example of South China craftsmanship. The true peranakan Chinese who had been brought up to appreciate the arabesque designs of Islamic art were not particularly fond of dragons, landscapes or grotesque figures of the Taoist pantheon. Besides, they have no specific uses for silver bowls in their customs other than as

commemorative objects of sentimental value. These bowls are clearly not in Straits Chinese taste.

Now there is no reason to believe that local Chinese silversmiths were unable to fabricate similar bowls of this type. After all Chinese silversmiths everywhere, whether in or outside of China, were all trained in the same tradition of craftsmanship. The scarcity of extant samples of such utensils in Straits silverwork clearly indicates that there never was any popular demand, even by the rich, for articles of this sort. There were, of course, lots of enamelled *porcelain* bowls of different shapes and sizes in peranakan homes, and some of them were beautifully painted and greatly treasured by their owners. Thus, while silver utensils as a whole may have been regarded as expensive luxu-

Fig. 118 The two plates shown here are of identical designs, and they were parts of a larger collection of silver plates and dishes originally commissioned for a prominent baba family in Malacca. The motifs, all in chased work, depict in concentric circular panels, a variety of marine objects including pikes, crabs and crustacea. A few squirrels are thrown in to add to the happy confusion of motifs which the 'Ching Fu' silversmith (so it is marked) characteristically delighted in! The flat rim is fluted on the surface and scalloped along the edges. Diameters of large and small plates: 14 cm and 10 cm respectively. Mark of 'Ching Fu'. From Malacca.

ries which only the more affluent peranakan families could afford, porcelain wares seemed to have been universally preferred for use on all important, festive occasions.

The same may be said of silver dishes and plates made by local Chinese silversmiths. There are very few examples of plates and dishes in existence, and even the handful of plates that have been traced to the heirlooms of well-known Straits Chinese families in Malacca, do not appear to be distinctively of peranakan taste. The designs of silver plates shown in figs. 117 & 118 come rather close to those of porcelain plates made to Straits Chinese specifications: there are the recognizable phoenix and floral motifs inside, especially the plate in fig. 117, while the narrow border around the rim is filled with the usual eight Buddhist emblems. The rim is scalloped. This plate (one of a pair) was specifically made for a Malacca family probably during the latter part of the nineteenth century, and is about the closest that any extant silver plate comes to Straits Chinese style of decorations.

As for the elegant little dish shown in fig. 26, we know that this utensil is of Straits Chinese craftsmanship. It was reputedly said to have been made in Johore. But notice that the flat but foliated rim, ornamented with what looks like trailing plum blossoms and executed in pierced work, is clearly reminiscent of celadon dishes made during the Ming Dynasty for export to the Middle East and Southeast Asia. There is every likelihood that this delightful dish was meant for some Malay client in Johore.

Fig. 119 This large oval dish weighing nearly 1.2 kilogram is unusual in size and design. It was obviously inspired by porcelain dishes made in European taste, except that the decorative motifs are entirely of Chinese origin. The principal motif in the centre of the dish is that of a large phoenix set amidst bamboos and peonies. The space in the cavetto is taken up with the flowers of the four seasons, bats, butterflies, frogs and insects, while the broad, flat rim is filled with an incredible profusion of fishes, seashells, prawns, cuttlefish, crabs, king crabs, tortoise, dragonflies and beetles. Mark of 'Ching Fu'. Length: 34 cm. Width: 27 cm. Height: 7 cm. From Malacca. Mariette collection.

Finally, the oval dish shown in fig. 119 is an exceptionally large silver utensil (it weighs over one kilogram) from a family heirloom in Malacca. It comes with a handsome but unusual ladle. The decorative designs are chased into the interior surfaces of the dish: the exterior surface is left plain. The main motif in the form of a huge phoenix is in the centre of the dish, and the cavetto is filled with boldly executed designs of flowers of the four seasons and lots of curious animals. The flat, broad rim is crowded with repoussé motifs depicting fishes, seashells of various types, prawns, cuttlefish, crabs, tortoise, dragonflies, beetles, etc. The stamped characters identify the maker as 'Ching Fu', reputedly said to have been a Cantonese silversmith in Singapore.

Ewers and teapots

As mentioned earlier on, it was not customary for the Chinese scholar-gentleman, even the most affluent of them, to serve tea from silver teapots. For one thing, Chinese tea connoisseurs (and in old China many a scholar-gentleman was a tea connoisseur in his own right) have always been unanimous in maintaining that tea brewed and served out of silver or, for that matter, any other type of metallic teapot, does not have the bouquet of real tea (see fig. 120). Besides, a silver teapot filled with freshly brewed tea soon becomes too hot and uncomfortable to handle with the bare hand. While silver teapots might have been regarded by wealthy merchants as status symbols, they did not particularly appeal to the traditional Chinese scholar. The brilliant and scintillating surface of all silverwares would most certainly have struck him as a form of vulgar ostentation. Yi-hsing wares, with their warm browns and subdued decorations, would have been far more preferable to members of the *literati* class.

During the Yuan Dynasty (1287–1368) when

Fig. 120 As will be seen in this illustration, silver teapots made to Straits Chinese taste share several common features, such as ornateness in the decorative motifs, diminutive sizes and compressed globular shapes. The two pumpkin-shaped teapots on the extreme right and left of the picture are exceptional in the beauty and simplicity of their multi-lobed, pear-shaped bodies. In fact they are both marked 'Ta Hing' and thus fabricated by the same firm of silversmith. Properties of various owners.

the Mongols ruled over much of China under Kublai Khan, that illustrious grandson of Genghis Khan, the use of large silver flagons, goblets, rhytons and bowls, which were noted in Marco Polo's descriptions of the court of Kublai Khan, was reserved for nobles, generals and other dignitaries of the court on all ceremonial occasions.[30] To the Mongols, gold and silver utensils were status symbols. From the viewpoint of the conservative mandarin officials of the imperial court in Peking, bred in the cultivated traditions of court etiquettes and Confucianism, however this Mongolian custom of using large gold and silver utensils was characteristic of uncouth barbarians who were typically given to flaunting their wealth and power.

Therefore the habit of quaffing wine out of large bowls or flagons was probably more fitting of uncultured people. The Chinese, on the other hand, from the most humble peasant to the emperor himself, had always preferred the use of delicate and diminutive porcelain utensils for both tea and wine-drinking ceremonies. For them elegance and gentility were the hallmarks of a superior culture. Now when it came to the customs and manners of the peranakan Chinese, we find, not surprisingly, that as a predominantly merchant and trading community, they indulged in conspicuous consumption namely to draw attention upon themselves. Even so, the silver artefacts made to their specifications have always

Fig. 121 These two distinctive teapots (originally parts of two wedding tea sets) are made in the shapes of pumpkins. However, the larger of the two has peony motifs appliqued to the multi-lobed surface of the teapot. The two utensils are stamped with the mark of 'Ta Hing'. Height of large teapot: 10 cm. Diameter: 10.5 cm. Height of small teapot: 6.5 cm. Diameter: 7 cm. From Malacca. Mariette et al.

been small and jewel-like in quality. For this reason most wine ewers and teapots made to peranakan tastes were crafted in the best traditions of ancient Chinese craftsmanship.

Incidentally, there is bound to be a little confusion over the distinction between a ewer and a teapot in discussions on Chinese silverwares. In the normal acceptance of the term, a wine ewer differs from a teapot only in respect of one feature, namely, the height of the body. The body of the wine ewer tends to be more elongated and ovoidal in shape than that of a teapot. Generally, a wine ewer is taller and more slender than a teapot. Chinese teapots, whether of gold, silver, enamel, porcelain or pottery, tend to be low and squat and either shaped like a pear, or generally of a compressed globular form. By this definition, then, the articles shown in fig. 121 *are* teapots, while those shown in figs. 126–128 must be regarded as wine ewers. Incidentally, I have been told by various nonyas that these elegant, antique silver wine ewers originally found in peranakan homes were never used for bouts of drinking by the babas

during wedding, birthday, Chinese New Year or any other festivities. On the contrary, they were highly venerated objects used only for making offerings on the ancestral table.

The shapes and functions of traditional Chinese teapots deserve some comments. Teapots, especially those specially made for the Straits-born Chinese were surprisingly small by European standards (see fig. 121). If you put one of these Chinese teapots beside those sumptuous eighteenth or nineteenth-century English and French silver teapots, you will be struck by the great disparity between the sizes of the Chinese and European teapots. Indeed, a Straits Chinese silver teapot looks more like an expensive bauble (and so it was!) than a functional and essential utensil of the peranakan bridal chamber.

As a matter of fact, the Chinese do have large teapots, some of which look like huge kettles and capable of serving up to fifty cups of tea! But such monstrous teapots were rarely seen in the homes of the wealthy and intellectual élites in China. The Straits Chinese certainly had no use for such large

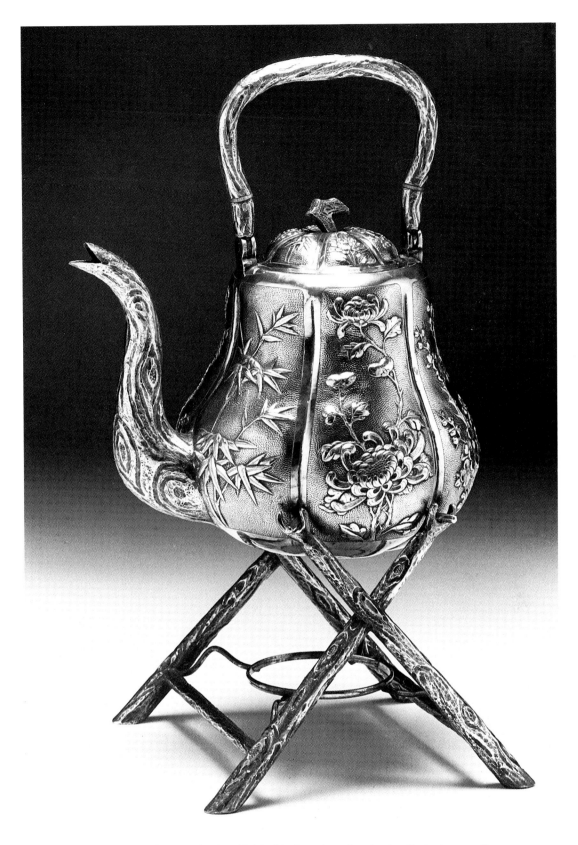

Fig. 122 This large tea-kettle with lobed body and overhanging handle, is shown resting on crossed supports simulating bamboo stems. It is a fine example of 19th-century China trade silver made for European markets, and assayed after the fashion of European silver-work. The motifs, executed in neat repoussé work, depict bamboos, peonies and lotuses. Probably of Shanghai workmanship. Height: 38 cm. Mrs. Ho Wing Meng.

teapots. There were several reasons why diminutive teapots were preferred to large ones. Firstly, a little teapot looks more elegant; and in the case of gold and silver teapots, smallness has the effect of making the article appear precious and more jewel-like. This appreciation for small but beautifully crafted objects is an aesthetic tradition which may be dated back to the T'ang Dynasty (A.D.618–906). Secondly, a small teapot is easy to handle and, in the opinion of tea connoisseurs, it retains the bouquet of good and aromatic tea far more effectively than a large and clumsy teapot. And thirdly, apart from the fact that silver has always been regarded as a precious metal in China and thus relatively expensive, it required special skill and a considerably longer time to fabricate an article of silver or gold. Most extant pieces of Straits Chinese silver teapots are barely 7 cm wide and 6 cm high.

Wedding tea sets

Most extant pieces of silvergilt teapots which come from old peranakan family heirlooms are usually found in pairs, and they are invariably accompanied by four conical-shaped teacups and a silver tray. These articles constitute what is known as 'wedding tea sets', because in the days gone by, such utensils were exclusively used for Straits Chinese wedding ceremonies which, among the rich, lasted twelve days. Thus a typical wedding tea set consists of a silver or silvergilt tray which may be square, circular, hexagonal or octa-

gonal in shape, two small, pear-shaped teapots richly ornamented with chased or repoussé work, and four conical-shaped teacups (see figs. 123–125). Since silver wedding tea sets were used only by the more affluent Straits Chinese families, they all tended to be crafted to a high standard of craftsmanship.

Notice, however, that in a typical Chinese tea set, there are no equivalents of the milk jar and the sugar bowl, simply because the traditional peranakan Chinese drank Chinese tea without sugar and milk. Nor, for that matter, do the teacups come with loop-handles and matching saucers after the manner of English and European teacups. While small, silver spoons – some of exquisite designs – were crafted from time to time, they were never used as *tea*spoons. Notice, too, that all the articles of the wedding tea set, with the exception of the tray, always come in twos or multiples of twos. Unlike the Japanese who regard odd numbers as lucky omens, the traditional Chinese (Straits Chinese not excepted) scrupulously avoided the use of odd numbers, especially with regard to all utensils, ornaments and pieces of furniture intended for wedding ceremonies.

Silvergilt wedding tea sets are among the most impressive examples of Straits silverwork. No expense was spared to ensure that these artefacts represented the paradigms of fine Straits Chinese craftsmanship. It is true that most of these tea sets are minuscule in comparison with their European counterparts, but the splendour and jewel-like quality of these articles (see fig. 124) often leave an indelible impression upon the mind of the beholder.

Fig. 123 Like all wedding tea sets made for the traditional babas, this set consists of two identical teapots, four cups and a matching tea-tray made in the shape of an octagon. The two compressed globular teapots are beaten out of rather thick silver plates and chased with a variety of animals, birds and floral motifs. The tray is particularly interesting: each of the eight sides is ornamented with a decorative panel of pierced work motifs which is appliqued to the side. The inside of the tray is engraved with peonies and a pair of phoenixes. Widest width of tray: 26.7 cm. No mark. From Penang. Mariette collection.

Fig. 124 This richly ornamented silvergilt wedding tea set comes with two pear-shaped teapots, four small European-styled teacups and eight miniature teaspoons of exceptional design. The spoons were probably not intrinsic to the tea set. The chased motifs on the teapots depict bamboos, prunus and pine motifs. Height of teapots: 6.5 cm. Diameter: 7.4 cm. Mark of 'Ching Fu'. Mariette collection.

Fig. 125 The wedding tea set shown here is unusual for having a well-raised, square tea-tray made from purple sandalwood inlaid with mother-of-pearl designs and ivory side panels ornamented in pierced work. Notice that the two teapots have disproportionately large lids with very prominent domes. The teacups are, however, delightful. From Singapore. Courtesy of Katong Antique House.

There is, however, some ambiguity concerning the real function of the wedding tea set in Straits Chinese wedding ceremonies. According to some people I have spoken to, the wedding tea set was exclusively intended for the use of the bride and the groom, and traditional peranakan customs required the bride to serve tea to her husband using the utensils provided by the wedding tea set. Another opinion has it, however, that among the Penang peranakans, such tea sets were used for the tea-serving ceremony, when it was the custom for the bride to serve tea to all her in-laws and elderly relatives at a special ceremony convened for this purpose. Whatever the truth of the matter may be – and Straits Chinese customs showed such wide variations – there is no doubt that the utensils of the wedding tea set could be used for either or both of these ceremonial functions.

As was to be expected, not every peranakan family could afford to use silver tea sets for their wedding ceremonies; the rare tea sets we illustrate here were heirlooms of well-to-do Straits Chinese families in Penang and Malacca. They were rare even during those halcyon years of the late nineteenth century, because most extant examples of wedding tea sets are made up of porcelain teapots and teacups held in dark red lacquer boxes. The set shown in fig. 123 is a paradigm case of accomplished workmanship, and it comes from Penang.

Wine ewers

If silver and silvergilt teapots are infrequently en-countered except in the homes of wealthy Straits-born Chinese, silver wine ewers are even rarer. I have not seen more than half-a-dozen pieces during the last twelve years or so. Only three wine ewers are being illustrated here.

The parcel-gilt ewer shown in fig. 126 was formerly part of the treasured heirloom of an old Straits Chinese family in Malacca. On stylistic considerations alone, its emphasis on figure and landscape motifs suggests that this ewer was probably fabricated by some master craftsman in South China and subsequently brought out to Malacca. Standing only 19 cm high, this wine ewer is decorated principally into six longitudinal panels around the elongated hexagonal, lobed body, somewhat simulating the style of vertical-scroll paintings. The predominantly repoussé motifs of the decorative designs are typical of Ch'ing period silverwork. Four of the panels depict scenes of armed horsemen and warriors riding out to battle, set against a background of awesome mountains; the two remaining panels, somewhat obscured by the positioning of the handle and the spout, show scenes of scholars and sages engaged in philosophical discussions and playing chess. The themes of these ornamental panels were probably derived from some significant events narrated in the *Romance of the Three Kingdoms*.

The consummate craftsmanship of this wine ewer is clearly evident in the artistry and technical refinement of the decorative motifs. The representation of the *ch'i-ling* which forms the finial of the cover is crafted with imaginative boldness and attention to detail.

Fig. 126 A wine ewer of superb craftsmanship – an heirloom piece from an old baba family in Malacca. The slightly lobed body is partitioned into six longitudinal panels, each of which is ornamented in repoussé work depicting figures of warriors and horsemen set against a mountainous landscape. The spout and handle are modelled after the manner of bamboo stems. Parcel-gilt. No mark. Height: 19 cm. Mrs. Ho Wing Meng.

Fig. 127 Wine ewer. Except for the handle, the spout and the lion finial on the cover, the decorative motifs are all executed in fine chased work. The four longitudinal panels are depicted with floral and foliated motifs, while the background is covered with fine latticed designs resembling the Buddhist swastika. Mark of 'Ching Fu'. Height: 16.5 cm. An heirloom piece from Malacca. Mariette collection.

There is a silver 'teapot' (it should be 'wine ewer') in the Victoria and Albert Museum, London,[31] which bears some resemblance to this ewer. It is of a truncated oviform shape, short and somewhat top-heavy in appearance. This is largely due to the large, domed cover, topped by a disproportionately large finial of twisted branches of the prunus blossoms. Each of the ornamental panels comes with a landscape scene, rather sparsely rendered and executed in low relief work.

The craftsmanship is of a high standard though it is not as elaborately or as meticulously finished as the ewer shown here. Besides, the truncated body gives the ewer in the famous British collection a rather squat and ungainly appearance. Nevertheless in its overall design, the British ewer resembles the Straits Chinese ewer in style and craftsmansip. The authorities in South Kensington date their ewer to around 1680. So if one goes by stylistic considerations alone, the Malacca ewer shown here should be given a late seventeenth-

Fig. 128 This elegant wine ewer of Persian design is reminiscent of those blue-and-white and copper-red porcelain ewers which Chinese potters made for export to the Middle Eastern countries from the fourteenth to the sixteenth centuries. The finely engraved designs on this ewer set against a dotted background are typical of Chinese art motifs of the T'ang Dynasty. Could we assign a Ming period dating to this ewer? Possibly not. Silvergilt. Height: 19.5 cm. From Singapore. Mrs. Ho Wing Meng.

or early eighteenth-century dating. But it was not, in all probability, a product of local silversmiths.

The remarkable ewer shown in fig. 127 also comes from a family collection in Malacca. It is very similar in shape and design to the ewer in fig. 126 except that its decorative motifs are entirely executed in fine chased work rather than relief work. The body is divided into six elongated, ovoidal panels, each of which is ornamented with one particular type of floral and foliated motif. The designs are so ornate and densely crowded together that one practically needs a magnifying glass to make out the details of the various motifs. The spaces outside these panels are covered with closely-packed latticed designs resembling the Buddhist swastika. The base is stamped with the mark of 'Ching Fu' (景福) and as this is reputedly said to be the name of a local silversmith whose firm became defunct long ago, we may infer that this ewer is the product of a local silversmith. It would also be dated to the late nineteenth century.

A MISCELLANY

There is one other type of Straits silverwork which must be mentioned here, although it was never used by the peranakan Chinese themselves. I refer to those sleeve ornaments (see fig. 129) which are modelled after the shape of a phoenix. According to several silversmiths in Johore and Malacca, these objects were apparently used as sleeve or shoulder ornaments for the bride and groom in traditional Malay wedding ceremonies. There is a pair of such phoenix ornaments in the collection of the National Museum of Singapore and it is described as 'Malay silverwork', although my information is that they were largely crafted by local Chinese silversmiths. In any case, the two pairs of ornaments shown in fig. 129 were products of Straits silversmiths, operating in Johore and Malacca. Phoenix ornaments of this type appear to have been confined only to the southern states of Johore, Malacca and Negri Sembilan. I have never encountered them in Perak, Penang or even Kedah.

The Straits Chinese versions of these phoenix ornaments, unlike those made in China, do not have long, graceful tails. Judging by the two pairs of phoenixes shown here, the locally made phoenixes were made of beaten silver. The details of the plumage are executed in chased work. And except for the head and the neck which are modelled in the round, the body, wings and tails are made out of broad, flat pieces of silver plates. On this point, it may be noted that there are no extant pieces of phoenix shoulder ornaments of local

origin which are decorated with the delicate blue feathers of kingfishers. Such pieces, whenever they are found, were formerly made in Peking, Shanghai or Canton for the home market.

Obviously my account does not exhaust the entire inventory of artefacts crafted by local silversmiths for various clients other than the peranakan Chinese of the Straits Settlements. The more discerning student of Straits silver, for example, will notice that I have not included in my illustrations those ornamental plates which resemble the shape of a necktie, and which come with birds and floral motifs (phoenixes and peonies?) executed in bold repoussé work. Such ornamental objects were used to adorn the bridal bed and were frequently found in Sumatra. In fact, they were used by the Sumatran royalty and nobility in the Padang–Bukit Tinggi area. I have also been told that similar pieces found in Malacca and Negri Sembilan were made for Malay clients of Minangkabau origin, that is to say, a tribe of the Padang–Bukit Tinggi area.

Then there are those head-dress ornaments (usually designed in the shapes of stylized flowers and birds) which, in the days gone by, were inserted into the ceremonial head-dress of Malay brides. Some years ago a Chinese silversmith in Malacca showed me a whole collection of such head-dress ornaments which he claimed had been made by his recently deceased father many decades ago. He did not wish to part with these head-dress ornaments partly because he treasured them as mementos of his father's handiwork, and partly because his Malay clients, including one royal family, regularly hired the entire set for their wedding ceremonies.

Fig. 129 The two pairs of sleeve or shoulder ornaments, designed after the fashion of some bird or phoenix, are reputedly said to have been affixed to the ceremonial costume of the Malay bridegroom. They are the handiwork of old Chinese silversmiths in Johore. Silvergilt. Length: 9 cm. Mariette et al.

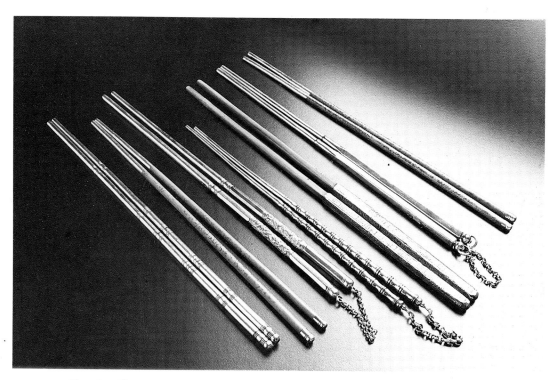

Fig. 130 The seven pairs of chopsticks shown here are no ordinary utensils: they were intended to be luxury articles (each set of chopsticks being individually hand-crafted out of pure silver and other luxury materials) and they were used only on special occasions. In traditional Straits Chinese customs, they were used only for worship. For this reason they are seen only on the ancestral altar-table or other tables used for worship. The babas did not customarily eat with chopsticks. Lengths vary between 20 cm and 23 cm. Mariette et al.

Another item deliberately omitted here is the amulet. Amulets, especially those made in the shape of a horizontal cylindrical box or, as sometimes seen, in the shape of a formalized bat or butterfly, had always been used in China to ward off evil. They were also commonly found in silversmiths in Singapore and Malaysia up to the early 'sixties. But for some reason which I have not been able to ascertain, amulets were rarely encountered among the usual *bric-à-brac* of Straits Chinese family heirlooms. We know for a fact that most of the traditional peranakan Chinese had been nominal Buddhists, Taoists and Confucianists. It appeared, however, that they did not take to wearing amulets or talismans as frequently as their China-born compatriots, the *sinkehs*.

I have, however, included some representative examples of silver or silver-plated *chopsticks* made to Straits Chinese taste in the illustrations (see fig. 130). Strictly speaking, chopsticks are quite alien to the culinary culture of the peranakan Chinese. This is due to the fact that unlike the traditional Chinese in China, the babas and the nonyas did not eat with chopsticks and bowls. They regularly ate with their hands after the manner of the Malays, the Indonesians and the South Indians. By all accounts, therefore, chopsticks had no useful function to play in a peranakan home. And yet we regularly find among the fascinating items of old, family heirlooms, a small but choice selection of finely crafted chopsticks made either of solid silver or ivory, ebony and bamboo sheathed in silver plates. There is in fact nothing plebian or cheap about Straits Chinese chopsticks.

We may presume, therefore, that these finely made chopsticks must have been intended for some formal or ceremonial uses. This assumption is correct; for my peranakan friends tell me that such chopsticks were usually placed on altar-tables beside offerings of food, fruits, cakes and

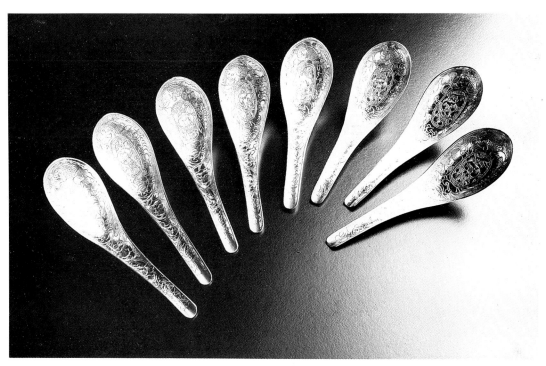

Fig. 131 Silver spoons have always been rare in Straits Chinese homes, mainly because porcelain spoons were more widely preferred and more greatly admired, especially by the traditional nonyas themselves. The eight spoons shown here are engraved with a variety of goldfish, crabs and peony blossoms, and came from an heirloom collection in Malacca. Mark of 'Ta Hing'. Length: 10.5 cm. Mariette collection.

Fig. 132 The dainty spoons and miniature forks shown here are not souvenir spoons and forks intended for tourists! They were crafted at about the turn of the present century, and the spoons were known as *ging-ging* or *longan* spoons. They were used for scooping dried *longan* boiled in water to make *longan* tea. The forks were used for nonya cakes. Length of spoons: 11.5 cm. From Singapore. Mariette et al.

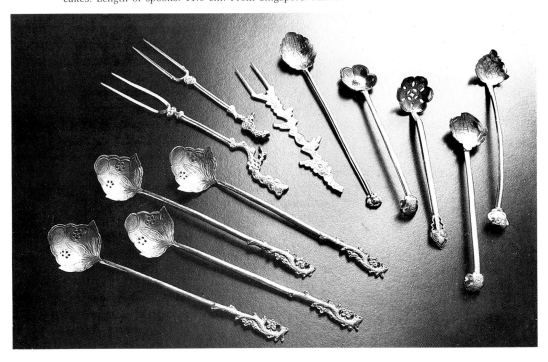

Fig. 133 A set of eight silvergilt spoons fashioned after the manner of porcelain spoons. The fine and delicate engravings depict a combination of floral and fish motifs. Length: 13 cm. Mark of 'Ta Hing'. From Penang. Mariette collection.

wine during All Souls' Day and the anniversaries of their deceased elders.

With regard to silver spoons (and these are not teaspoons), they too are few and far between. But they are nevertheless beautifully crafted (see figs. 124 & 132); some have ornamental scoops which resemble leaves or flower petals. They must not be confused with *tea*spoons, because the traditional Straits Chinese never drank tea with sugar and milk after the fashion of the English. What, then, could they have been intended for? Ornamental teaspoons were usually given as wedding presents, and in those bygone days, such dainty-looking spoons were used for scooping dried *longan* fruits which had been boiled with water to make *ging-ging* tea – a sweet which the peranakan served during birthday festivities. These spoons may also have been used to serve glutinous rice balls boiled with water and *gula melaka* (a brown sugar made from fermented coconut juice) during wedding celebrations.

Those remarkable silver spoons shown in figs. 131 & 133 have been modelled after the standard shape of porcelain spoons. But whereas porcelain spoons, especially the variety painted in *famille rose* enamels to cater to Straits Chinese taste, are fairly common, silver spoons are rarely seen. They are, of course, quite different from the more delicate and fanciful *ging-ging* spoons, being larger and more sturdily constructed. They are said to have come from an heirloom collection in Penang, and may be dated between the late nineteenth and early twentieth centuries. There is no evidence at all to show that these spoons have been regularly used in the past, because they are in such a pristine state of preservation – no scratches, no worn-out patches, no patina. They look as if they were made only yesterday.

Two rare and unusual categories of Straits silverwork, namely, covered jars (or *kamchengs*) and small incense burners, should be mentioned here, if for no other reason than to underline the

Fig. 134 A silver *kamcheng* pot is one of the rarest objects in Straits Chinese silver, though there are hundreds of porcelain *kamchengs* in extant. The floral and foliated designs with magpies are all executed in fine chased work. The neat key-fret borders on the cover and the collar of the pot, together with the *ju-i* border on the shoulder, add considerable poise and dignity to an otherwise ordinary utensil. An heirloom piece from the Tan Kim Seng collection. Height: 22 cm. Widest width: 15 cm. From Malacca. Private collection.

surprising range of artefacts crafted by local silversmiths of what is now a bygone era. The silver *kamcheng* pot shown in fig. 134 is one of the most exceptional pieces of silverwork I have seen in more than a decade. **Porcelain** *kamchengs* are fairly common, and come in a variety of sizes and colours. But who has heard of a **silver** *kamcheng*? This one originally belonged to the Tan Kim Seng collection in Malacca. The decorative motifs, following the trend established in Straits Chinese porcelain, depict a pair of phoenixes and blos-soming peonies executed in neat and precise chased work. It is stamped with the mark of 'Ching Fu'.

The little incense burner (see fig. 135) with tripod legs is a fine example of craftsmanship in miniature. The four panels of decorative motifs executed in repoussé work are so crisp and precisely delineated that they clearly betray the hands of a master silversmith at work. It is stamped with the mark of another noted silver-smith, namely, 'Ta Hing'.

Fig. 135 This tub-shaped, miniature incense burner is unusual, not only for the basket-weave patterns chased on to the outside of the body, but also for the spindly tripod legs with gargoyle-like masks. The designs inside the decorative panels are executed in repoussé work. Parcel-gilt. Height: 6.5 cm. Mark of 'Ta Hing'. From Singapore. Author's collection.

5 Dating and Attribution of Straits Chinese Silver

STUDENTS OF EUROPEAN silver wishing to acquire Chinese silverwork for the first time, and who happen to be familiar with the Western tradition of dating and assaying silverwork, are bound to be disappointed when they discover that antique Chinese silver artefacts, no matter where they originated, are not dated and assayed according to the practice of traditional European guilds of goldsmiths and silversmiths. To begin with, they will not find, except in very rare instances, equivalents of the *nien haos* or imperial reign marks that one regularly finds in antique Chinese porcelain wares, bronze objects and cloisonné work. There are no cyclical marks, hallmarks, commendation marks or symbolic marks of any sort to provide the scholar with clues for the dating and attribution of Chinese silverwork. Besides, there was no equivalent in China of a state or government institution known as the 'Assayer's Office', whose job it was to certify that the content of the silver (or gold) used in the fabrication of any artefact met the required standards of purity prescribed by the state authorities.

Thus, the novice of antique Chinese silver faces, at the outset, two difficulties which he will gradually learn to overcome, as he familiarizes himself with the traditional Chinese concept of artistic excellence. He will learn to recognize that from the standpoint of Chinese connoisseurship, the value of an antique object does not depend upon the intrinsic nature of the material out of which it was made nor, for that matter, the sheer antiquity of its age. Rather, it is dependent upon artistic excellence and craftsmanship. For this reason, provided an antique object is technically well-made and artistically praiseworthy, it does not matter at all what material it is made from, nor how far back in time the article might be dated.

Now the absence of European methods of assaying and marking did not, however, prevent traditional Chinese silversmiths from devising their own system of marking and authenticating their products. Indeed one frequently finds in most pieces of Chinese silverwork stamped characters of two sorts: (1) those which denote shop-names, and (2) those which purport to state the quality of the metal used, such as 'Pure Silver', represented by 足銀 or 'Chu Yun', and 纹銀 or 'Wen Yun'. However these substitute for proper assayer's marks of recognized guilds or state institutions, it should be stated here that they are not to be taken at their face value, unless there are other independent criteria of corroboration, such as, for example, other stamped marks giving the names of some well-known and long-established silversmith noted for the quality and reliability of their products and the usual acid-and-scratch tests on the jeweller's black stone, to determine the purity of the metal employed. Pieces which happen to be stamped with the numerals '80' or '90' in addition to the 'Chu Yun' and 'Wen Yun' are, without doubt, the products of old Hong Kong and Shanghai silversmiths, and they may be dated between the second half of the nineteenth century and possibly the first two decades of the present century.

As every student of antique Chinese porcelain knows from experience and hearsay, the mere presence of some date and/or reign mark on a piece of antique pottery or porcelain article is not to be taken as authenticating evidence of the real age of the object. This is because there was an ancient tradition in Chinese ceramics dating back to the Ming Dynasty (1368–1644) for the emperor to send down orders to the Director of the Imperial Kilns in Ching-tê-chên in Kiangsi Province to make copies of some ancient pieces which he favoured, and such specially commissioned imperial pieces could be intended for the emperor's birthday, the anniversary of his ascent to the throne, or any other auspicious ocasion. This tradition was still in vogue during the Ch'ing Dynasty, and the Emperor Yung Chêng (1722–36) used to send regular orders, together with samples of fine porcelain taken from the imperial collection, to Nien Hsi-yao, the talented Director of Works in Ching-tê-chên, so that reproductions of these older wares could be made for the emperor's household use. Usually, these pieces would be marked with the names of the reigning monarch even though the style of the porcelain designs belonged to an earlier period. To complicate matters, some of the reign marks of the earlier emperors were sometimes used in the reproductions.

Now this habit of making reproductions or, if you prefer, deliberate fakes, especially when decreed by the emperor for use in the royal household, was not meant to deceive anyone, and students of ceramics soon learned how to distinguish the originals from the later reproductions. And over the years, students of Chinese ceramics developed a knack for detecting stylistic dif-

ferences between the original objects and their later copies. Thus the rules which apply to techniques for the dating and attribution of Chinese ceramics apply equally to the methods of authenticating other types of ancient arts and crafts. And the same may be said about the dating and assaying of a piece of antique Chinese silver. For occasionally one may chance upon a piece with the characters 足銀 stamped on the base, but which turns out to be a forgery when other tests are applied to authenticate the purity of the metal. In fact the silver content of many extant pieces of Straits silverwork is no higher than 85 and 90 per cent. Some are even lower. The Malay term for the more highly alloyed silverware is 'Perak Assam'.

The bulk of modern Indonesian silver tea services, especially those made in Jogjakarta in Central Java, in imitation of baroque Dutch silverware, is strictly 'Perak Assam'. Several years ago, while on a visit to Jogjakarta, we were taken to a factory where Javanese craftsmen turned out intricately ornamented tea services. To our inquiry concerning the silver content of these pieces, one of the craftsmen replied unhesitatingly that it was between 40 and 50 per cent.

This does not mean that *all* antique Chinese silverwares which are stamped with the standard 'Pure Silver' mark are fakes, though it can be quite disconcerting to an unwary collector if he happens to buy an attractive piece of antique silverware which, upon verification, turns out to be a form of alloyed silver. This absence not only of reliable assayer's marks, but of a uniform standard in the consistency of the silver, may be attributed to the fact that silversmiths of the former Straits Settlements, as well as those in other parts of Southeast Asia, unlike their European counterparts, had never been organized in guilds which jealously guarded their reputation by strictly imposing a consistent standard of quality for all artefacts which are stamped with their own hallmarks. It is true that the clannish Chinese had their associations of goldsmiths and silversmiths, but there is no evidence whatever that these associations were ever supervised along the lines of European guilds, or even that they exercised the same stringent regulations with regard to the purity of the metal and the standard of the craftsmanship. And in the absence of powerful guilds which zealously guarded their reputation for quality work, the temptation among the smaller and more obscure silversmiths, most of whom operated small-scale family concerns, to adulterate the silver, or to offer products of shoddy quality, was strong – especially if their clients were not overly critical in their purchasing habits.

Nevertheless students of Straits silverwork need not be deterred by the difficulties associated with the absence of some Bureau of Standards for marking and assaying silverwork. After all some of the more reputable silversmiths in the Straits Settlements had been noted for the quality of their craftsmanship and the purity of the metal they employed to fabricate all their products. And if the potential student or collector of Straits silver values the craftsmanship and artistic excellence of a piece of silverwork, it should not matter too much that the silver content of an artefact is not 92.5 per cent pure, or that its age is not at least 100 years old. Besides, we know from all available evidence that the bulk of Straits silverwork found in family heirlooms of old Straits Chinese homes, in pawnshops and in established silversmiths in Malaysia and Singapore, may be dated only as far back as the nineteenth century. For it was during this period that the peranakan community attained its zenith of prosperity; large quantities of silver (and gold) ornaments, jewellery and other objects of *virtu* were turned out to meet the requirements of the well-to-do and ostentatious nonyas. We know, too, that by the opening decades of the present century, the art of the Chinese silversmith had declined so markedly that many traditional craftsmen were forced out of work.

Although most extant pieces of Straits silverwork are the products of nineteenth-century workmanship, one occasionally encounters some odd pieces (see fig. 128), which would appear on stylistic considerations to pre-date the nineteenth century. This is not particularly surprising as (a) the Chinese had an ingrained habit of perpetuating a tradition of craftsmanship for hundreds of years on end without change, and (b) the Straits Chinese community had been living continuously in Malacca for six hundred years. It is not unreasonable to assume that some silver artefacts of Chinese workmanship must have been made long before the nineteenth century. Is there objective evidence of a circumstantial sort which one might apply to determine the real or ostensible age of these archaic-looking silverwork? There are, theoretically speaking, at least four broad categories of circumstantial evidence that one might take into account. They are:

(1) the evidence of local history concerning the origins of the peranakan Chinese in Malacca as well as the cultural peculiarities relating to their customs and traditions;

(2) any *bona fide* information given by owners of family heirloom pieces, and/or the testimonies of old established goldsmiths and silversmiths concerning the age or origin of these artefacts;

(3) the application of the well-known method of 'parallel dating' whereby the ostensible age of any artefact is computed on the assumption of its being contemporaneous with other objects with which it happens to be associated, and which happen to be more easily datable, as in the case of archaeological findings; and

(4) stylistic evidence based on comparative affinities and differences between a piece of Straits craftsmanship and artefacts which are authentically attributable to the products of Chinese silversmiths of different periods.

Let us look briefly at some of the sources of information and see if we can glean some helpful clues concerning the origin and development of Straits silverwork. The first thing to note is that records of the origins and evolution of the baba community and their distinctive culture which were purportedly written by the peranakan Chinese themselves are non-existent. As has already been indicated in an earlier chapter, the Straits Chinese did not evolve a written language of their own, nor, for that matter, did they learn to read and write in the native language of the Malays, namely, Jawi. They had a *spoken* language known as Baba Malay which had no written form until the last two decades of the nineteenth century, when a few peranakan scholars began translating ancient Chinese classics and *pantuns* or ballads into Baba Malay.

As for the evidence of local history, the relevant data available to us are not any more enlightening either. The scanty reports of early travellers to Malacca are sketchy, episodic and based on hearsay. However, we learn from the official records of the Ming Dynasty, *Ta Ming Hui Tien*, that the history of the Straits Chinese community spans at least six hundred years. Until the fifteenth century, most of the Chinese traders in Malacca did not set up permanent settlements; and even after the Portuguese conquered the city in 1511, the Chinese community was a small and insignificant one, as far as numbers were concerned.

We have no records as to when the earliest artisans and craftsmen, especially goldsmiths and silversmiths, came from China to settle in Malacca. But all the available evidence shows that with the rapid decline of the power and influence of the Dutch East India Company in the coastal states of the Malay Peninsula towards the end of the eighteenth century, and the subsequent founding of Penang in 1786 to be followed by the founding of Singapore thirty-three years later in 1819, the influx of Chinese immigrants into the former Straits Settlement colonies gained in momentum. The records of the Dutch authorities, however, showed that there were Chinese 'artisans' in Malacca when the city fell into their forces in 1641.

Many of the older generations of Straits Chinese can still recall with a sense of pride that their community flourished during the nineteenth century, and it is to this period, therefore, that they attributed some of the finest cultural objects unique to their community, including fine silverwork. In this respect, too, we have the authority of Dr. Bo Gyllensvard who refers to all those examples of Chinese gold and silverwork executed in typically high relief work as 'Cantonese work' which, according to him, became the popular and predominant technique for executing the decorative designs of gold and silverwork of the latter part of the Ch'ing Dynasty.[32] The silversmiths who operated in the Straits Settlements were largely Hokkien or Teochew craftsmen, though there were some Hakka and Cantonese craftsmen among them.

However, one occasionally encounters a piece of silver artefact among Straits silver collections which, on stylistic grounds, would appear to be of greater antiquity than one would normally have expected. Indeed there is no reason, theoretically speaking, why the earliest pieces of Straits silverwork should not be dated back to the sixteenth century, during the flourishing era of Portuguese supremacy over Malacca. The problem, however, is that even assuming there were Chinese silversmiths working in Malacca during this period, it is unlikely that any of their works would have survived the upheavals which subsequently overtook the city. The Portuguese and the Dutch fought long and bitter wars to gain control of the spice trade by dominating Malacca and the vital shipping route, namely, the Straits of Malacca. In any case, we have no authenticated evidence of Straits silverwork in extant which can be dated as far back as the sixteenth century.

The absence of any authenticated sixteenth-century Chinese silver artefact may also be accounted for by the irresistible urge of people to melt down even the most priceless and irreplaceable works of art in times of war and civil disorder. Many of the goldsmiths and silversmiths with whom we broached the subject of antique silver, told us that it had always been their practice to melt down gold and silver ornaments to recover their bullion value as soon as they went out of fashion, irrespective of their artistic excellence or cultural value. Unlike porcelain which has no intrinsic value once an antique pot is broken and reduced to a heap of shards, gold and silver ornaments can always be melted down to extract the value of these precious metals. Therefore, pawnshop owners as well as goldsmiths and silversmiths, being shrewd businessmen, were primarily concerned with the saleability of their arts and crafts. This, more than anything else, accounts for the non-existence of any silver artefact datable to the sixteenth century, if indeed there were already silversmiths working in Malacca at this early period of its history.

There remains, then, the seventeenth century which has not yet been accounted for thus far, as the next likely period to which the beginnings of Straits silverwork may be attributed. Here again there are several factors which mitigate against the seventeenth century as the period most conducive to the growth and development of the leisurely art of silver craftsmanship. The first half of the seventeenth century was marked by a period of open hostilities between the Dutch and the Portuguese as the former tried to wrest the control of the spice trade from the hands of the Portuguese. This resulted in considerable disruption to the lucrative trade between Malacca and the Spice Islands in the East Indies, the embargo on Chinese junks trading with the city, [33] and a drastic reduction in the population of Chinese traders, many of whom fled from Malacca at the height of the hostilities between the two contending European powers.

Since the founding of Batavia (the former name for Jakarta) in 1619, the Dutch East India Company (which was fully backed by the Dutch government) had been making repeated attempts to dislodge the Portuguese from the control of the spice trade, by systematically attacking Malacca, or by blockading the trade routes through the vital waterway of the Straits of Malacca. In 1641, after more than a decade of systematic attacks on all foreign vessels plying in and out of Malacca, and alternately besieging the city, the Dutch finally stormed and captured it from the Portuguese. By then the population of Malacca which, at the height of the Portuguese era had stood around 20,000,[34] dwindled down to 2150 according to Purcell.[35] Out of this, no more than 300 or 400 were Chinese.

Malacca was left in ruins, and from then on never again recovered its former greatness as the premier trading post in the Far East. The Dutch imposed strict controls on the movements of all ships coming into and going out of the city *via* the Straits of Malacca. Chinese junks from China were forcibly prevented (at gunpoint!) from sailing to Malacca; so it was not until the last quarter of the eighteenth century when the British East India Company began to gain ascendancy in the Far East, that the Dutch lost control of the Straits of Malacca when they were forced to give up Malacca during the Napoleonic Wars in Europe. By 1750 the Chinese population in Malacca had grown to 2160, whether through natural increase, or immigration, no one seemed to know.

If, for the sake of argument, we assume that the remnants of Straits silverwork somehow escaped the upheaval and destruction of those decades before and after the fall of Malacca to the Dutch during the seventeenth century, we would still have no way of telling which among those extant pieces of Straits silver can be attributed to this period, for reasons already alluded to. The fact is that most cultural artefacts peculiar to the Straits Chinese community may be datable only as far back as the eighteenth century at best. Practically nothing going back to the seventeenth, or even the sixteenth century, appeared to have survived the passage of time. *For this reason, we are perhaps on firmer ground in assigning the bulk of Straits silverwork to the late eighteenth and nineteenth centuries.*

In attempting to date Straits silverwork purely on stylistic considerations, one must of course take into account the fact that the Chinese craftsman worked in a very conservative tradition; the same style of craftsmanship with regard to forms and decorative motifs is often repeated through several hundred years without change or innovation.

Parallel dating is based upon the assumption that some silver artefacts which we are attempting to date are closely and contemporaneously

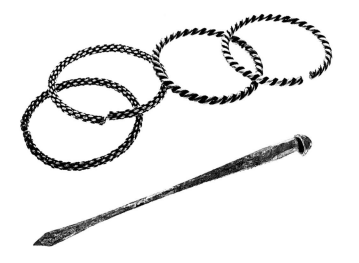

Fig. 136 For years I have been told by various people that the traditional baba-nonyas buried their dead with some of their personal jewellery and ornaments, silver ornaments in particular. But it was not till fairly recently that I was given the opportunity of examining buried objects exhumed from graves in a Hakka cemetery in Singapore. The two pairs of bracelets and single hairpin were said to have been recovered from different graves dated to about the turn of the present century. Length of hairpin: 14 cm. Author's collection.

associated with some other objects whose age can be determined by independent tests. For example, if we happen, by chance, to stumble upon some old, nonya-styled hairpins in a grave which was recently exhumed, we can determine the age of these hairpins with sufficient accuracy by finding out when the wearer of these hairpins died according to the inscriptions carved on the tombstone. Unfortunately, as far as Straits silverwork is concerned, it is extremely rare that one gets an opportunity to put this criterion to the test. Firstly, although Straits silver artefacts must have formed part of the grave furniture of the deceased Straits nonyas in the days gone by, it is not common for Chinese graveyards in most parts of Malaysia to be exhumed to make way for new roads, railway lines or new buildings. It was only in Singapore in recent years that several cemeteries were exhumed to make way for urban re-

newal projects. I was recently given an old silver hairpin and two pairs of bracelets (see fig. 136) which had been recovered from one of the old graves exhumed along Holland Road some years ago. But since the identity of the grave from which this hairpin was taken could not be ascertained, there was no way of telling the age of the hairpin. All that we know about this cemetery is that the oldest tombstones bore inscriptions bearing the name of the Emperor Tao Kuan (1820–50) of the Ch'ing Dynasty, while the most recent of them were dated to the 1920s.

It is certain that the traditional peranakan Chinese buried their dead fully clothed and adorned with all the paraphernalia for an afterlife, including gold and silver ornaments. But the bulk of extant Straits silverwork that has survived to this day was never interred with the bodies of their original owners, but instead passed down the generations as treasured mementos of a bygone era. Secondly, the bulk of private collections of antique Straits Chinese silverwork came from old pawnshops, junk stores, antique shops and private homes, so that by the time these artefacts reached us, they had already passed through several hands, thus making it virtually impossible to trace them to their original owners.

Old Straits silverwork is generally tarnished with a thin but very hard coat of blue, bluish-black or grayish black patina. Even the gilded pieces are similarly tarnished after a certain period of time, though silvergilt is more resistant to tarnishing than untreated white silver. Provided, therefore, that such pieces of Straits silverwork have not been tampered with, the presence of the dark, resistant patination is a good indication that such specimens are of vintage craftsmanship. However, whenever an apparently genuine piece of old Straits silver is displayed in an antique shop for sale, the chances are that it would have been stripped clean of every trace of old patina to give it a new and gleaming appearance. Obviously when this happens, one can no longer rely upon the presence of patination as a rule-of-thumb guide to determine the antiquity of the piece of silverwork. One would then have to resort to other features in the artefact such as the style of the workmanship and the contents of the decorative motifs, to help determine its true provenance.

Fortunately for the student of Straits silverwork, the practice of faking the craftsmanship of old and bygone local silversmiths has not caught on yet, as it has with old Indonesian silverwork (especially the old Palembang and Jogjakarta silverwares) which have been widely reproduced in Jogjakarta and Jakarta. Most of these pieces are being aged with a blackish enamel in the interstices of the repoussé and chased work to enable them to pass off as antique work. While there has been a growing interest and awareness in the cultural uniqueness of Straits Chinese silver in recent years, there is no evidence that modern fakes are being fabricated in Peninsular Malaysia. Except for the Malaysian government's laudable attempt to revive the dying craft of silverwork in Kelantan (and Kelantan silver is largely of filigree or chased work executed in strict Islamic or arabesque motifs) the art of the Chinese silversmith is a thing of the past. The modern generation of goldsmiths who operate in Singapore and Malaysia have neither the patience nor, I must add, the ancient skills of their forebears, to turn out works that once graced the persons and the homes of the Straits Chinese nonyas.

Apart from that, Straits silverwork is largely unknown and unheard of outside Singapore and Malaysia. Until very recently, local students of Chinese antiquities, even though they had been aware of Straits silverwork, looked upon such artefacts as junk, unworthy of serious consideration. This is not particularly surprising, because gold and silverwork has always been regarded in China as a very minor craft – the works of artisans rather than true artists. And so by a curious conspiracy of circumstances, silverwork has always attracted little attention. It must also be borne in mine that the reproduction of old silverwork is a long, tedious and demanding craft.

There is no point spending days, weeks or even months crafting a piece of silverwork (assuming one had the requisite skill and training) for which there is no immediate demand.

As noted previously, the fashion of wearing elaborate silver ornaments and jewellery became obsolete some sixty or seventy years ago. This, and the fact that in these days of premium labour costs coupled with increasing emphasis on the acquisition of well-paid scientific and technological skills, make it practically impossible to induce anyone to resuscitate a craft which involves long apprenticeship and meagre rewards. Any person or company which contemplates the setting up of a viable business of turning out modern reproductions of old Straits silverwork will have to face the prospects of offsetting his profit-margins against the high labour costs – not to mention the crucial difficulty of hiring people with the requisite skills for the job.

Thus, for all practical purposes, the deliberate faking of old Straits silverwork is a non-viable business proposition, not simply because there is little demand for these things, but also because the tradition of fine silver craftsmanship in Malaysia and Singapore has been lost beyond recall. Let me, however, dilate a little more on this matter about the lost art of Straits silverwork.

Most of the older generation of silversmiths whom we have spoken to during the past twelve years intimated that it was an open secret to everyone familiar with the business, that in the past the master craftsmen (the *sai pehs*) always made it a rule not to reveal some of the finer and more recondite aspects of their skills, even to their most devoted and talented pupils. This rule

of secrecy was strictly adhered to, presumably so that the master could never be surpassed by his disciples. The only instance in which this rule might be relaxed was when the master and pupil were related by bonds of kinship, such as father-to-son, or uncle-to-nephew. In all other circumstances, the *sai pehs* tended to guard their secrets with the zeal of Rosicrucian or Sufic mystics.

The practice of guarding trade secrets with jealous fanaticism in ancient China applied not only to goldsmiths and silversmiths, but also to master craftsmen and professional savants of other forms of highly marketable skills, such as the making of pottery and porcelain, silk-weaving, bronze-casting, jade-carving, furniture-making, herbal medicine, martial arts, etc. In a country where poverty had always been rampant, people who happened to have acquired some special skills or useful knowledge through guilds, great good luck or sheer hard work and native intelligence, were naturally wary about sharing their expertise with others.

For those well-intentioned people to whom the policy of free and open dissemination of knowledge and skills through public discussions, conjectures and refutations, the publication of books and journals, was an academic necessity, this niggardly Oriental habit of harbouring what might turn out to be information of practical and theoretical importance must seem deplorable. But it must be borne in mind that in a vast and ancient country where copyrights and patent-right laws were unknown, and where the universal enforcement of laws and regulations had always been highly problematical, the only recourse open to any person in possession of some high marketable skill (if that skill also happened to be his sole means of earning a livelihood) was deception and secrecy.

The Chinese have a long tradition of reverence for scholarly talent and a healthy appreciation of good books; and people with unusual talents or in possession of important knowledge had always been aware of their responsibility to preserve and to transmit their intellectual legacies to posterity. For this reason, some of these savants had taken the trouble of recording their ideas and expertise in writing, even though their manuscripts were accessible only to their sons and members of their immediate families and remained closed books to the world at large. If this, too, is frowned upon, one may perhaps plead that Confucianism, which prescribes one's loyalty to, and responsibility for, ensuring the welfare and continued survival of one's own family, outweighs all other obligations a man might have.

And so we must sympathise with those 'selfish and crafty' old silversmiths who, if they had not already transmitted their trade secrets to their sons, carried their knowledge and expertise to their graves. Straits silverwork may indeed have become an extinct art. But fortunately, there has been no scramble to buy up even the remnants of antiquated artefacts, either by local collectors or museums throughout Malaysia and Singapore. Connoisseurs of Chinese art regard these things as 'minor arts', while students of native Malay arts regard Straits silverwork as artefacts of foreign origin. The chances of buying fakes are therefore remote. Nonetheless, the disappearance of what must once have been an enormous quantity of Straits silverwork may be attributed to the ingrained habit of commercial-minded silversmiths and pawnshop owners in melting down vast quantities of these artefacts for the purpose of recovering their bullion value. I do not know of instances where large quantities of old silverwork have been hoarded by dealers and antique collectors.

For the aspiring student of Straits silverwork: all things being equal then, the darker and more resistant the coating of patina on an apparent old piece of silverwork, the greater is the age of the article in question. But it cannot be over-stressed that no single characteristic feature by itself is a reliable guide, either to the authenticity or antiquity of a piece of old silverwork. Where Straits silver is concerned, there is the further question of identifying its stylistic peculiarities. But if the reader has come this far with us, he would, by now, have a fairly good idea of what a typical piece of Straits silver looks like.

Shopmarks

As previously noted, Chinese silverwork was rarely dated according to the traditional system of imperial *nien haos* that one finds in porcelain, bronze, cloisonné and lacquer work dating from the Ming to the end of the Ch'ing Dynasty. This is also true of Straits silverwork which is simply stamped with the Chinese equivalents of European assayers' marks, namely, 'Wen Yun' or 'Chu Yun' (足銀) both of which simply mean 'Pure Silver'. In addition to these marks, one occasionally finds pieces which are also stamped with the shop-names of various goldsmiths and silversmiths in which these artefacts had originally been crafted. It should be noted here that the names stamped on these articles are not the signatures of the craftsmen themselves. It was not the custom in China for craftsmen, potters, sculptors and artisans to inscribe their names on their works simply because they were not permitted to do so. All artisans were regarded as people of low social status, and therefore expected to remain anonymous, irrespective of whether their handiwork was widely recognized for excellence of craftsmanship. For this reason, it was usually the firm to which a particular craftsman was employed which took the credit and the reputation for its employees' handiwork. Of course the services of experienced and talented craftsmen were highly valued by their employers, and they generally received higher remunerations. Still the fact remains that in ancient China artisans, unlike artists and calligraphers, were never accorded the status and recognition traditionally reserved for members of the intellectual élite. We may presume, therefore, that such names as 'Ta Hing' (大興), 'Tien Hing' (天興) and 'Ching Fu' (景福) – to mention but three of the more notable firms of Straits silversmiths – which collectors of Straits silver occasionally encounter in the better quality pieces, are in fact shop-names rather than the names of the craftsmen themselves.

According to Mrs. B. Mariette, a noted collector of Straits silverwork, the firms of 'Ta Hing', 'Tien Hing' and 'Ching Fu' were local silversmiths whose products were well-known for refined craftsmanship, and whose patrons included at least two prominent and wealthy peranakan families in Malacca. She said that she had noted, over the last several years, that some of the treasured heirloom pieces which had formerly been part of the collections of several Straits Chinese families in Penang and Malacca, were stamped with the marks of one or another of these three silversmiths. While I have not been able to trace the sources of some of these articles to their original owners, I did notice all along (as I pointed out on page 54 of the First Edition) that the better quality pieces of Straits silverwork are indeed stamped with the names of 'Ta Hing' and 'Ching Fu'. That at least two notable Malacca families regularly patronised the products of the 'Ta Hing' and 'Ching Fu' silversmiths during the latter part of the nineteenth century, confirms my suspicion all along that these exquisite works of art must have been made for patrons who appreciated superb craftsmanship and were prepared to pay high prices for them. So different were they from those run-of-the-mill pieces.

Those distinctive pieces stamped with the marks of 'Ta Hing' or 'Ching Fu' which I first encountered more than ten years ago in the course of various trips to Johore, Malacca and Penang, had all been found in silversmiths, antique shops and pawnshops. It was virtually impossible, therefore, to try and trace the origins of these artefacts back to their owners, not merely because it was the habit of local dealers and pawnshop owners to withhold information concerning their sources, but also that the vendors themselves made it a condition of their sale transactions that their real identities would remain secret. Nonetheless, as I came to handle more and more samples of Straits silverwork, it became clear to me that those finer pieces of *buntal* plates, curtain hooks, belt-buckles, *sireh* boxes and teapots, judging by the distinctive quality of their workmanship, were intended for discriminating clients of means.

This observation was further strengthened by an unstated principle of Straits Chinese connoisseurship, namely, that good taste was determined not by the sheer magnitude of any particular artefact, but rather by the sheer refinement of the craftsmanship. For this reason, while a wealthy peranakan might, say, wear a set of belt-and-buckle which, to all intents and purposes, looks very similar to another set worn by another peranakan of more modest means, the former's articles of personal ornaments may nevertheless be distinguished from the latter's by the subtle and more artistic qualities of the workmanship and, perhaps, by the intrinsic value of the metal employed – in this instance, the use of gold rather than silvergilt.

Thus, there was never any doubt in my mind that those items of Straits silverwork bearing the 'Ta Hing' and 'Ching Fu' marks surpassed all other extant pieces in beauty and precision of craftsmanship.

We are now fairly sure that the 'Ta Hing' and 'Tien Hing' silversmiths were of local origin and, according to the information we have been able to cull from old silversmiths in Singapore, they once operated their establishments like many other silversmiths, along Arab Street, Jalan Sultan, and North Bridge Road. 'Ta Hing' was said to have become defunct a long time ago, but no one nowadays seems to know exactly when the firm closed its doors for the last time. We do not know either whether 'Ta Hing' had subsidiaries in Johore Bahru or Malacca, but I would not be surprised at all if it had operated in Malacca Town, since quite a few pieces of silver artefacts stamped with the 'Ta Hing' marks have been traced back to the heirlooms of a couple of prominent and wealthy families in Malacca.

'Tien Hing' was perhaps not as well-known as 'Ta Hing' and 'Ching Fu' during those halcyon years of the nineteenth century. But among the better pieces of Straits silverwork may be included a few samples stamped with the marks of 'Tien Hing'. The older generations of craftsmen who had once worked for this firm have disappeared from the scene, but the firm is still operating a little goldsmith shop in Blanco Court, North Bridge Road, under the name of 'Tien Hua'.

Locating the whereabouts of the 'Ching Fu' silversmith in Singapore presented something of a problem. Surprisingly, no one among the surviving generation of silversmiths along the Arab Street–North Bridge Road area was able to say whether the 'Ching Fu' silversmith had an establishment in Singapore. They seemed to have heard of it, and recognized the name as belonging to what they thought was a Cantonese or Shanghainese silversmith. My own guess, based purely on circumstantial evidence, is that the 'Ching Fu' silversmith was probably located in Malacca. The strongest evidence in favour of this view is that many of those extant pieces of Straits silverwork stamped with the 'Ching Fu' marks (see figs. 119 & 127) appeared, on careful investigations, to have originated from the heirlooms of several prominent and well-to-do Straits Chinese families in Malacca. Even in those instances where these articles had been found in Singapore or Penang, it was still possible, in a number of cases, to trace the sources of these heirloom objects back to Malacca, especially if the last owners happened to be related to, or were descendants of, some families in Malacca.

If we look at the matter from the viewpoint of those wealthy Malacca clients in those bygone times when transport and communications were so much slower, there is no doubt that it was more convenient for them to commission some reputable but locally-domiciled firm of silversmith, to fashion all their silver utensils and items of personal ornaments, rather than having to send to Singapore or, for that matter, Penang, to have their silverwares crafted. And since many of those extant examples of silver stamped with the 'Ching Fu' marks could be traced to the collections of at least two prominent Malacca families, the available evidence clearly points to Malacca as the probable *locale* of the 'Ching Fu' silversmith.

It is unlikely that the 'Ching Fu' silversmith was located either in Hong Kong, Canton, Amoy or even Shanghai for the following reasons: Firstly, most of the articles made in Canton, Hong Kong and Shanghai from about 1850 to 1900, and intended for export to Europe and America, were generally crafted to European tastes – the only Chinese characteristic permitted being the motifs employed in the ornamental work. Secondly, since such articles were intended for European clients, they had to be assayed after the manner of European silver-work. They are thus stamped with such numerals as '800', '850' or '900' (sometimes '80', '85' or '90') to indicate the purity of the metal employed. They also stamped the names or initials of the silversmith in English. Occasionally the provenance of the piece is indicated by the names 'Hong Kong' or 'Shanghai' on the base of the article. Later pieces (usually twentieth-century pieces that is) may simply be assayed by the use of the word 'Sterling' or 'Sterling Silver' with the numerals '800', '850' or '900'.

None of those extant pieces of silverwork bearing the 'Ching Fu' marks are, however, marked and assayed after the fashion of European silver. There are no English words or Arabic numerals stamped on their works; instead you will find a set of Chinese characters giving the name of the silversmith and another set of characters denoting 'Pure Silver'. As for the artefacts made by the 'Ching Fu' silversmith, the motifs are essentially of Chinese origin, while the shapes may be either traditionally Chinese or Sino-Malayan in style.

One final observation: practically all extant pieces of silverwork bearing the 'Ching Fu' marks show definite consistency in (1) the choice of decorative motifs employed, namely, a decided preference for fishes, crabs, prawns, shells and other marine fauna, (2) the characteristic style of depicting the designs, and (3) a tendency to employ the technique of chased work more frequently than that of repoussé work. I interpret this consistency of style and theme to indicate that all existing artefacts bearing the 'Ching Fu' marks were the handiwork of one particular master craftsman.

Notes

1. Ling Roth, *Oriental Silverwork: Malay and Chinese* (London: Truslove and Hanson, 1910).

2. Frank Swettenham, *British Malaya* (London: 1907).

3. H.N. Ivor Evans, 'Malay Arts and Crafts' 1923, *Malayan Pamphlets* (Malay Studies Information Agency: 1924).

4. R.O. Winstedt, *Malaya* (London: Constable and Co., 1923).

5. *Ibid.*, p.111.

6. I am aware that local peranakans spell the word *nonya* as *nyonyas. Nonya* is the way it is spelt in Jakarta, though not in Singapore or Malacca, and I have adopted the Indonesian spelling out of sheer habit.

7. Lim Huck Tee and Wijasuriya, D.E.K., *Index Malaysiana* 1878–1963 (*Journal of the Malayan Branch of the Royal Asiatic Society,* 1970).

8. A.H. Hill, 'Kelantan Silverwork', *JMBRAS,* 1951.

9. J.M. Gullick, 'A Survey of Malay Weavers and Silversmiths in Kelantan in 1951', *JMBRAS,* 1952.

10. These include J.D. Vaughan's *The Manners and Customs of the Chinese of the Straits Settlements,* 1879 (reprinted by Oxford University Press in 1953); Sir Song Ong Siang's *One Hundred Years of the Chinese in Singapore,* 1923 (reprinted by University of Malaya Press, 1967); Victor Purcell's *The Chinese in Malaya,* Oxford University Press, 1948; and several interesting articles, which appeared in the *New Nation,* 1973, concerning the babas; and a couple of academic exercises by Mrs. Rosie Tan and Miss Diana Wong, available in the Main Library of the National University of Singapore.

11. The following description of the Chinese by T.J. Newbold is also typical of nineteenth-century English opinion: 'The character of the Chinese may be summed up in a few

words. They are active, industrious, persevering, intelligent, educated sufficiently to read and write, and to use the swampan or reckoning board (abacus?). They are entirely free from prejudices of caste and superstition, which are grand stumbling-blocks to the natives of India. On the other hand they are selfish, sensual, ardent lovers of money, though not misers; inveterate gamblers, and often addicted to smoking opium. The Chinese will expose himself to all dangers for the sake of gain, though he would not stir a finger to save a drowning comrade . . . '. From *Political and Statistical Account of the British Settlements in the Straits of Malacca* (London: John Murray, 1839), 13.

12. J.D. Vaughan, *The Manners and Customs of the Chinese of the Straits Settlements*, 1879.

13. A well-known lady from Malacca once said to me that when she and her sister returned from England after having spent a good many years studying in London (?), her father who was himself essentially English-educated, would not hear of his daughters adopting the newfangled way of life and the Christian religion, and insisted that they should revert to the traditional customs of the baba community. It was not till much later that he relented and recognized his daughters' rights to adopt Western customs.

14. Victor Purcell, *The Chinese in Malaya*, 1948 (Reprint. Oxford University Press, 1967).

15. A friend recalled that he visited Malacca some twenty-five years ago when he was still a young man, and was put up in the home of a well-known family living in Heeren Street. A couple of days after his arrival he was introduced to an elderly lady of the house who calmly looked him up and down for a few moments and then said: 'Ba, are you a "china"?'
Somewhat taken aback by this unexpected question my friend replied, 'Why, yes, "beebik" (a polite term for addressing all nonyas), but aren't *you* also a "china" like me?'
'No, I am a "peranakan" (i.e., Straits-born person),' the old lady replied in a matter-of-fact tone of voice.

16. The babas also objected to the term 'chinaman' on the ground that, strictly speaking, it was a violation of the English grammar much in the same way that 'Englandman' is an ungrammatical expression.

17. While it is true that the Straits babas had been recognized as British subjects since 1826, the British colonial government had never in fact formally and legally accepted their status as such. Indeed none of the babas who subsequently went abroad for further studies, whether in England or the United States, were ever issued with British passports. They were only given Certificates of Identity, and these, too, were formally issued in 1844. Sir Song Ong Siang, in his *One Hundred Years of the Chinese in Singapore*, drew attention to this legal sleight of hand which he considered a grave anomaly in British justice.

18. For a more detailed treatment of the peculiarities of the baba language, see W.C. Shellabear, 'Baba Malay', *JMBRAS*, 1913.

19. Preface to *An English-Malay Dictionary* (Singapore: Malaya Publishing House, 1916).

20. This statement must be qualified somewhat. It is true that there is hardly anything which might be dignified with the title of 'Straits Chinese literature' in the sense of original literary compositions composed by baba writers. Since the publication of the First Edition of this book in 1976, I came to discover, much to my surprise and delight, that there is a body of literature written in Baba Malay which I had not hitherto known about. Mr. William Tan, an accomplished singer and *pantun* reciter in the Gunong Sayang Association of Singapore, showed me a whole collection of ancient stories going back to the Yuan Dynasty, including such famous classics as *Romance of the Three Kingdoms,Water Margin, Madam White Snake, Pavilion of Ten Thousand Flowers*, and at least twenty-five other titles, all translated into Baba Malay and published in Singapore (!) as far back as 1892. These Chinese classics, including some stories of the Kung-fu type, were translated by peranakan scholars of which the most well-known were Mr. Chan Kim Boon and Mr. Wan Boon Seng. Mr. Chan Kim Boon who went by the pen-name of 'Batu Gantong' ('Hanging Rock' that is) undertook the translation of the *Romance of the Three Kingdoms* into 30 volumes under the title of 'Chrita Dahulu-Kala Nama-nya Sam Kok atau Tiga Negri Ber-prang'. He took four years, from 1892 to 1896, to complete the translation work. Mr. Wan Boon Seng translated *Pavilion of Ten Thousand Flowers* under the title of 'Hikayat ini bernama Ban Wha Law' into 12 volumes in 1911. I also learnt from Dr. Philip Lee Thomas of the School of Human Communication, Murdoch University, Western Australia, that the National Library of Singapore possesses two out of four volumes of a collection of *pantuns* supposedly written by peranakan Chinese. I have not seen this collection, but I have been told the British Library possesses the other two volumes missing from the National Library of Singapore.

21. According to Dr. Chêng Tê-kun, vide *Archaelogy of Sarawak* (Cambridge: University of Toronto Press, 1969), 3-4, Admiral Cheng-ho led seven great maritime expeditions into the Indian Ocean. The first expedition consisted of an armada of sixty-two large ships, each of which was 440 feet long and 180 feet wide, with four decks and hundreds of watertight compartments. These ships were accompanied by 225 ships and they carried a total of 28,000 men! This was probably the largest armada in history, and for nearly thirty years they sailed across the Indian Ocean and back, and even reached as far as the coast of Africa at least a century before the coming of the Portuguese.

    T.J. Newbold, in *Political and Statistical Account of the British Settlements in the Straits of Malacca* (London: John Murray, 1839), 122, attributed the foundation of Malacca to Sultan Sri Iskandar Shah. According to him, 'Malacca was founded in the middle of the thirteenth century, by a colony of Malays, from Singapore, under the sovereign of that Island, Sri Iskandar Shah, who had been driven thence by an invasion of the Javanese from Madjapahit.' Prof. P. Wheatley and others, particularly Tome Pires, regarded Parameswara as the founder.

22. Purcell's *The Chinese in Malaya*, 20-22.

23. 'The Chinese of Malacca', *Historical Guide of Malacca*, Printers Ltd., Singapore, 1936, 71-83.

24. Schuyler Cammann, *China's Dragon Robes* (New York: Ronald Press, 1952), chap. 1, p.4.

25. Queeny Chang, *Memories of a Nonya* (Singapore: Eastern Universities Press, 1981).

26. Many nonyas whom I interviewed agreed that the advent of the modern *sarong kebaya* came about this time.

27. See Plate XII of Christiane Desroaches-Noblecourt's *The Life and Death of a Pharaoh: Tutankhamen* (Penguin Books, 1965). Plate II showing the pectoral is described as 'one of the richest jewels of the treasure'.

28. *Ibid.*, pp. 145-6.

29. Ho Wing Meng, *Straits Chinese Porcelain* (Singapore: Times Books International, 1983).

30. Kublai Khan, according to Marco Polo, used to reward his nobles and high-ranking military officers 'by presenting many with vessels of *silver*, as well as the customary tablets or warrants of command and of government. The tablets given to those

commanding a hundred men are of silver; to those commanding a thousand, of gold or silver-gilts; and those who command received ten thousand tablets of gold bearing the head of a lion.' (p. 161).

'In the rear of the body of the palace there are large buildings containing several apartments, where is deposited the private property of the monarch, or his treasure in gold and silver bullion, precious stones and pearls, *and also his vessels of gold and silver plate.'* (p. 169).

Marco Polo also mentioned 'a capacious vessel, shaped like a jar, and of precious materials, calculated to hold a tun . . .' and vessels of hoghead, cups and flagons of 'gilt' (apparently silvergilt) in the grand court. From *Travels of Marco Polo*, Everyman edition, 1954. Intro. by John Masefied. J.M. Dent, London.

31. See article by Sylvia Coppen-Gardner, entitled 'Chinoiserie Silver' in *Discovering Antiques*, pp. 404–907.

32. *Chinese Gold and Silver in the Carl Kempe Collection* (Stockholm: Nardisk Rotogravr, 1953), 47–8.

33. The strategic importance of Malacca, lying as it does along the route from the Spice Islands of the Moluccas and the Malay Archipelago to the Middle East and Europe, was recognized by the Portuguese early in the sixteenth century. As Prof. Paul Wheatley puts it: 'During the fourteenth century the Strait was the crucial sector of the world's major trade route which had one terminus in Venice – or even further westwards — and the other in the Molucca Islands. Spices were carried through the Archipelago over many routes and ships of diverse peoples . . . before finally entering the Middle East through either the Persian Gulf or to the Red Sea, but to the Straits of Malacca there was no practicable alternative. Here the staple produce of the Archipelago was funnelled through a natural channel in places less than forty miles wide. This, as the later Portuguese were to realize, was the only point through the 8000 miles of trade route at which a monopoly of spice distribution could be established.' *The Golden Khersonese* (Kuala Lumpur: University of Malaya Press, 1961), 312–3. Malacca in those days served as the collecting centre for the exchange of spices and other products of the Archipelago for the staple manufactures of India, particularly the textiles of Gujarat, Coromandel, Malabar and Bengal. From the Moluccas and the Bandas came nutmegs, maize, Borneo camphor, sandalwood, lignum aloes, bensoin, musk, seed-pearls, batiks, Javanese krises and bird plumes.

34. If one includes the population of the hinterland as well.

35. Purcell's *The Chinese in Malaya*.

Glossary

À jour **setting** According to European jewellers, the method of *à jour* setting for gems came into fashion in Europe during the tenth century A.D. In the method of *à jour* setting the base plate of a piece of jewellery is omitted, and the stone is clasped in position by a ringed metal frame which is open both on the top and the bottom. This method of mounting gems was used only for those jewels which were of greater purity and brilliance. The more flawless the gem, the more beautiful it is when mounted in *à jour* setting.

Areca nut Areca nuts come from the areca nut palm, *Areca catechu*. This palm is native to most parts of Southeast Asia. Areca nut is also referred to as 'betel nut'.

Bekas sireh The Malay term for a special container, usually crafted in silver, made for holding *daun sireh* or *sireh* leaves. *Bekas* simply means a container.

Betel vine The betel leaf or *daun sireh* is obtained from the betel vine (*Piper bette*) which is commonly found all over Southeast Asia.

Box-setting Box-setting is an ancient method of mounting jewels, especially those gems which are cut *en cabochon*, that is to say, the top side is ground and polished to a dome shape while the underside is ground flat. To mount *en cabochon* gems, goldsmiths and silversmiths made little ring-shaped frames and soldered them onto the base of a jewelled article. The stones are then embedded into the frames and the rings are then hammered inward until the various gems are firmly held in position. The older variety of Straits Chinese jewellery is characterized by the frequent use of box-setting for the mounting of all its gems.

Chased work Chasing is the opposite of the repoussé technique. In chasing, the metalsmith usually begins by drawing or tracing the outlines of the decorative design on the surface of a sheet of silver. Having done this, he then places the silver sheet on a matrix of pitch or resin face upwards, and begins to hammer out the design with punches and small hammers. Chasing is also known as 'low relief work', and it is usually combined with repoussé work and engraving.

Chelpa The Malay term for a tobacco box. In the days gone by, the Malays (as well as the babas and nonyas of the Straits Settlements) regularly chewed finely shredded tobacco, just as they did *sireh* leaves flavoured with lime, gambier and areca nuts.

Chimbul The Malay term for a box used exclusively for holding finely sliced pieces of areca nuts.

Diamond Diamond is the hardest substance known to man. It is made up of pure crystalline carbon. The rarity of diamonds is legendary, and for sheer lustre and brilliance it has no equal. Most of the diamonds in the world today come from South Africa, although some famous, legendary diamonds were originally found in India. The Koh-i-Noor diamond which now forms part of the British crown jewels, was discovered in Golconda, India. The Shah diamond, weighing 88.70 carats, the Arcot diamonds and the Orloff diamonds weighing 199.60 carats, were all found in India. Diamonds come in various colours: the best and most expensive are the blue diamonds (e.g., the Hope Diamond in the Smithsonian Institution), bluish-white diamonds, yellow diamonds and light brown diamonds shading to cinnamon colour. As far as Straits Chinese jewellery is concerned, it was customary for those who belonged to the wealthy merchant class to have all their jewellery set in diamonds, blue sapphires and green emeralds. Such diamond-studded jewellery of archaic designs, are, however, rarely seen nowadays. Most extant pieces are simply mounted with pearls or a variety of rough-cut industrial diamonds.

Electro-plating This refers to the application of a coating of pure silver to an article (usually copper or nickel) by electrolysis. The technique of electro-plating was invented by Henry Elkington of Birmingham in 1840. In electro-plating, minute particles of silver are deposited on the article to be plated, producing a coating of pure, unalloyed silver which is hammered all over to close all the pores and produce an even surface. When the hammering has been completed the surface is polished. EPNS, meaning 'Electro-plated nickel silver', is a kind of silver-plated ware which was produced in large quantities during the nineteenth century in Sheffield and Birmingham, England, as a cheaper substitute for silverware.

Enamelling Enamelling is a technique of decorating gold and silverwork by the use of masses of coloured glass which are applied to those decorative areas which have been specially prepared by cloisons, and heating the enamel in a muffle furnace at 700–800°C. In order to make the coloured glass powder stick to the surface of the metal, a vegetable or resin bonding agent is used. Enamelling is, however, rarely used in Straits Chinese silver. In ancient China, from about the time of the Sung Dynasty, Chinese jewellers used blue kingfishers' feathers to decorate jewellery.

Engraving The technique of engraving on gold and silver consists of using a sharp-pointed steel graver for scratching on the surface of a sheet of gold or silver. Where it is necessary to make the engraved designs stand out more clearly, metalsmiths and jewellers usually rubbed black substance or enamel into the fine grooves carved out by the graver. Engraving is rarely used in Straits Chinese silver.

Filigree and granulation work The word 'filigree' is derived from the Latin term *filium* meaning 'wire'. Filigree work, therefore, is a technique of decorating any article, utensil or item of jewellery by soldering pieces of wires of different lengths to create aesthetic designs. Usually, the various lengths of wires are twisted into spirals, tendrils and lattices, and soldered onto the surface. Filigree designs are usually combined with granulations. Granulation (from the Latin term *granum*, that is, granules or droplets) consists of soldering little blobs, granules or particles of gold and silver onto the surface of an article. In traditional Chinese gold and silverwork filigree designs are combined with appliqué motifs as well as granulation. Some Straits Chinese brooches are entirely executed in granulation work. Granulation work is also referred to as 'granulé work'. In European continental usage the term 'granulé' is used more frequently.

Gambier This is an astringent extract taken from the leaves of the gambier tree, *Uncaria gambir*. The juice is usually solidified into little cubes or balls.

Gilding Gilding is a very important technique of goldsmithing widely used in China and even the Straits

Settlements during the nineteenth century. There are three different ways of gilding less valuable metals so that they can be made to look like gold: (1) cold gilding; (2) firing; and (3) chemical gilding. In cold gilding, very thin sheets of gold foils can be pasted onto a metal surface in successive layers until the base metal takes on the appearance of real gold. In more modern times, goldsmiths employ chemical electro-plating to cover a silver article with a thin layer of gold. The thickness of the gilding is measured in microns, say, 20 microns, or 40 or 60 microns. Finally, the third method of gilding is fire-gilding. In fire-gilding, a certain amount of gold is dissolved in mercury and then painted over the surface of the silver article and then fired. The mercury vaporizes and leaves behind a hard layer of gilding on the surface.

Gold, Au Gold is a very dense, yellow metal of brilliant lustre. It is found in telluride ores and usually found among veins of quartz and pyrite. The chief gold-producing countries are South Africa, Soviet Russia, Canada and the United States. Gold is highly valued not simply for its rarity but also for its unique physical properties. It is of high density (19.3 times the weight of an equal volume of water), great ductility and malleability, and is highly resistant to corrosion. It does not oxidize in air; it is not dissolvable in most alkalis and pure acids, though it dissolves in *Aqua regia* (a mixture of one part nitric acid and three parts hydrochloric acid) and cyanide. Gold has been the symbol of wealth in all civilizations of man in recorded history. Pure gold is described as '24 carat' whereas alloyed gold may be described as 12, 14, 16, 18 or 22 carats. The reddish hue of Chinese gold is due to the addition of small quantities of copper.

Intans The commonest type of semi-precious stone used for embellishing brooches, hairpins, pendants, bracelets, and earrings in Straits Chinese jewellery, was an irregularly-shaped, semi-transparent stone mined from the towns of Banjermasin and Pontianak in Kalimantan. In Baba Malay, such stones are known as 'intans', while in the Hokkien dialect they are called 'swan p'ik'.

Niello work *Niello* work is an archaic form of enamelling, except that the black enamel used here is not glass enamel but a mixture of silver, copper, lead, sulphur and borax, applied to the chased or engraved designs on a piece of silver artefact and then melted in a weak fire to produce that characteristic blackish background. The *niello* technique of enamelling decorative metal wares is no longer used in Europe although it is still commonly employed in India and Thailand. The word *niello* comes from the Latin term *nigellus* meaning 'blackish'. During the nineteenth century, Malay silversmiths were particularly fond of using this technique of decoration for their silverwork.

Repoussé work Repoussé work refers to a particular technique of decorating the surface of a sheet or plate of silver (and gold as well) by the use of steel punches of various shapes and sizes. In applying the repoussé method of working, the silversmith usually begins by tracing or drawing the decorative designs on the back surface of a sheet of silver. Next he places the sheet face downwards on a bedding made of pitch or resin (substances which are moderately firm yet yielding) and hammers out the outlines of the designs with the help of small hammers and steel punches. The repoussé technique is also described as 'embossing', 'embossed work' and 'relief work'.

Silver, Ag Silver is a soft, lustrous white metal which is highly malleable and even more ductile than gold; one gram of pure silver can be drawn into a thin wire more than a mile long, and silver foils can be beaten into 0.00025 mm in thickness. Silver is usually found in *Argentite* ores, but it also commonly occurs among ores containing copper, nickel, lead and zinc. Nowadays the bulk of silver produced comes from the United States, Canada, Mexico, Peru, Australia and Spain. Silver is a high conductor of electricity and heat. It dissolves easily in nitric acid and its melting point is 960°C. A light-weight metal, it is easily available and at least 40 times cheaper than gold. The main drawback of silver is that it oxidizes and tarnishes when exposed to air; so that before long all silver articles become coated with a dark brown or bluish deposit of silver sulphide. Like gold, pure silver is far too soft to be worked into utensils and items of jewellery; so it is usually alloyed with copper to give added strength and stiffness to these articles. In Britain and Europe since medieval times, the amount of copper or other adulterating metals which may be added to pure silver without depreciating the value of silverwares is between 8 and 10 per cent. Guilds of Silversmiths and Governmental Bureau of Standards assay all items of silver to ensure that the precious metal content does not deviate below 900 or 925 grains of silver per 1000 grains. Sterling silver, for example, is said to be '925/1000' or 92.5 per cent pure silver.

***Sireh*-chewing** Mr. Mubin Sheppard (see his *Taman Indera*, Oxford University, K.L., 1972) makes the interesting claim that the habit of chewing *sireh* leaves with small quantities of lime, gambier, dried cloves and areca nut, originated in Malaya more than a thousand years ago. This custom, according to him, was said to have been carried to India, the Philippines and Arabia (what about Indonesia?) by Malay sailors. My own impression is that *sireh*-chewing originated in South India, and that this custom was brought over by Tamil merchants and traders to Southeast Asia as far back as the Srivijaya Period (between the seventh and eighth centuries A.D.). There is, however, no recorded evidence for verifying either of these two claims. As far as the peranakan Chinese of the Straits Settlements are concerned, there is no doubt whatsoever that they adopted the habit of *sireh*-chewing from the Malays of Malacca.

***Sireh* containers** The term refers to those globular covered boxes and cups used for holding areca nuts, gambier, cloves, lime. This term is also used interchangeably with 'betel-nut boxes'.

Tempat sireh The Malay term for a rectangular, circular, square or hexagonal box, used to contain the following articles (i.e., circular boxes, cups, a pair of shears, and triangular container) used in *sireh*-chewing. The box itself may be made of lacquered wood, inlaid purple sandalwood, solid silver, silver and tortoiseshell, ivory, or silver-plated nickel. There is no standard shape for the *tempat sireh*, but the babas and nonyas regularly preferred a lidless rectangular box which is partitioned into an L-shaped and rectangular compartment, and a little concealed drawer directly beneath these compartments. *Tempat sireh* literally means 'a container for *sireh*'.

Bibliography

Bo, Gyllensvard. *Chinese Gold and Silver in the Carl Kempe Collection.* 1953.

Cane, Richard. *Silver.* London: Octopus Books, 1972.

Chan , Kim Boon (otherwise known as Batu Gantong). *Chrita Dahulu-Kala Nama-nya Sam Kok, atau Tiga Negri Ber-prang.* Vols. 1–30. Singapore, 1892.

Chan, Kim Boon. *Chrita Dahulu-Kala di triak Song Kang, atau 108 p'rimpak di zaman Song Teow.* Vols. 1–19. Singapore, 1899.

Coppen-Gardner, Sylvia. 'Chinoiserie Silver', *Discovering Antiques:* 404–907.

Durdik, Jan. *The Pictorial Encyclopaedia of Antiques.* New York: Hamlyn, 1970.

Evans, H.N. Ivor. 'Malay Arts and Crafts', 1923, *Malayan Pamphlets.* Malay Studies Information Agency, 1924.

Gullick, J.M. 'A Survey of Malay Weavers and Silversmiths in Kelantan in 1951', *Journal of the Malayan Branch of the Royal Asiatic Society.* 1952.

Hill, A.H. 'Kelantan Silver', *Journal of the Malayan Branch of the Royal Asiatic Society.* 1952.

Ho, Ruth. *Rainbow over my Shoulder.* Singapore: Eastern Universities Press, 1975.

Ho, Wing Meng. *Straits Chinese Porcelain.* Singapore: Times Books International, 1983.

Holland, M. *Phaidon Guide to Silver.* Oxford: Phaidon, 1978.

Newbold, T.J. *Political and Statistical Account of the British Settlements in the Straits of Malacca.* London: John Murray, 1839.

Pang, Teck Joon. *Hikayat ini bernama Ban Wha Law cherita yang susah dari hal 'Teck Cheng' di zaman Song Tiow Raja Jin Chong.* 10 vols. Singapore, 1910.

Purcell, Victor. *The Chinese in Malaya,* 1948. Reprint. Oxford University Press, 1967.

Roth, Ling. *Oriental Silverwork: Malay and Chinese.* Reprint. Oxford University Press, 1910.

Scott, Hugh. *The Golden Age of Chinese Art.* Tokyo: Charles E. Tuttle, 1967.

Shellabear, W.C., 'Baba Malay', *Journal of the Malayan Branch of the Royal Asiatic Society.* 1913.

Shellabear, W.C., *An English-Malay Dictionary.* Singapore: Malaya Publishing House, 1916.

Sheppard, Mubin. *Taman Indera* (Malay Decorative Arts and Pastimes). Kuala Lumpur: Oxford University Press, 1972.

Song, Sir Ong Siang. *One Hundred Years of the Chinese in Singapore,* 1923. Reprint. University of Malaya Press, 1953.

Swettenham, Frank. *British Malaya.* London, 1907.

Tan, Chee Beng. 'Baba Malay Dialect', *Journal of the Malayan Branch of the Royal Asiatic Society.* Vol. 53, Part I: 150–66.

Vaughan, J.D. *The Manners and Customs of the Chinese of the Straits Settlements,* 1879. Reprint. Oxford University Press, 1953.

Watson, William. *The Genius of China* (Catalogue of an exhibition of archaeological finds of the People's Republic of China, held in the Royal Academy, London, September 1973–January 1974).

Wheatley, Paul. *The Golden Khersonese.* Kuala Lumpur: University of Malaya Press, 1961.

Williams, C.A.S. *Outline of Chinese Symbolisms and Art Motives.* Shanghai: Kelly and Walsh, 1932.

Wilson, H. *Silverwork and Jewellery.* Pitman Publishing, 1973. Originally published in 1902.

Winstedt, R.O. *Malaya.* London: Constable and Co., 1923.

Yeap, Joo Kim. *The Patriarch.* Privately published, 1975.

Yeh, Hua Fen. *The Chinese of Malacca.* Historical Guide of Malacca. Singapore: Printers Ltd., 1936.

Index